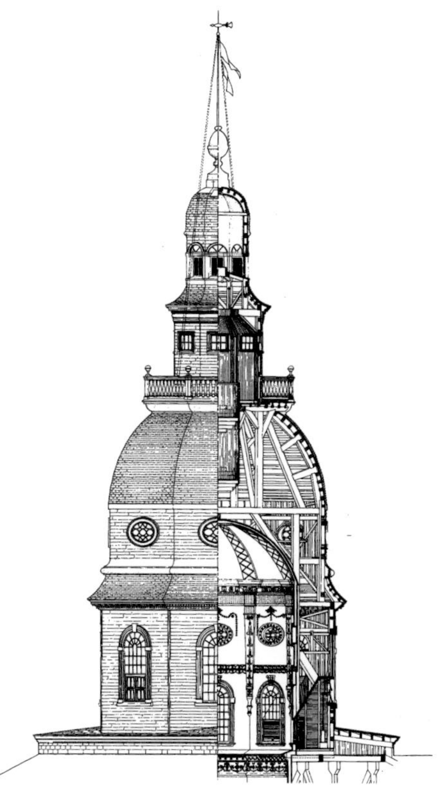

The Maryland State House

250 YEARS OF HISTORY

Mimi Scrivener Calver

THE MARYLAND STATE ARCHIVES AND
THE FRIENDS OF THE MARYLAND STATE ARCHIVES
JUNE 2020

**THE MARYLAND STATE ARCHIVES AND
THE FRIENDS OF THE MARYLAND STATE ARCHIVES**

DESIGN BY MICHELE A. DANOFF, GRAPHICS BY DESIGN

**ANNAPOLIS, MARYLAND
JUNE 2020**

ISBN 978-0-942370-63-8
Library of Congress Control Number: 2020908349

Table of Contents

Inside front and back covers:
Elevations of Maryland State House,
Charles Willson Peale, 1788.

Introduction

When approaching Annapolis, by land or by water, the distinct white octagonal dome of the State House is a beacon to visitors and residents alike. It has defined the skyline of this historic city since the late eighteenth century, and, although other architectural features have arisen over time, no other landmark has been more closely associated with Maryland's capital city. The State House dome is the icon of Annapolis.

State Circle, on which the building stands, encompasses 325 years of Annapolis history. It is the highest point in the city and has been the heart of Maryland government since the capital was moved to Annapolis from St. Mary's City in 1695. The current State House, the third built on this site between 1772 and 1779, is the oldest State House still in continuous legislative use in the nation—its elected occupants moving seamlessly from the "old" chambers into their "new" chambers added onto the building in 1904. From early January until mid-April, these rooms, now themselves over a century old, are filled with the bustle and business of the annual legislative session.

The co-existence of these "old" and "new" chambers distinguishes Maryland's State House from other capitols in Colonial-era states. In most cases, when an original state house became too small or unsuited for the business of its government, a new capitol was built, leaving its predecessor to become a museum—if it escaped demolition. In Maryland, we are fortunate that the "old" and the "new" co-exist in one extraordinary building, offering our visitors the opportunity to travel through more than three centuries of Maryland history.

Our State House is further distinguished as a National Historic Landmark, due to the events of 1783–84, when the Confederation Congress met here at the end of the Revolutionary War and some of the most important events of that time took place in the Old Senate Chamber. In fact, the war officially ended here with the ratification of the Treaty of Paris on January 14, 1784, making Annapolis, and this State House, the first peacetime capital of the new United States of America.

In authoring this first comprehensive volume, Mimi Calver has compiled decades of research by archivists, historians, and curators, along with historical and contemporary photography, to document thoroughly the history of the Maryland State House in one accessible volume. This is the first guidebook to the history of the building's architecture, as well as its artwork, furnishings, and exterior grounds. The research that is the foundation of this book is an important legacy of retired State Archivist Dr. Edward C. Papenfuse, whose own scholarship, and that of the many staff he mentored, painstakingly documented the history of the State House, its collections, and the events that occurred here.

The Maryland State Archives is proud of its long association with the interpretation and preservation of the State House. Since 1969, with the establishment of the Maryland Commission on Artistic Property, the Archives has cared for the historic works of art and furnishings here, as well as developed the interpretive exhibits which have evolved over the years.

Most recently, under the auspices of the State House Trust, the Archives led the implementation of the Visitor Experience Master Plan that includes the restoration of the historic chambers, the creation of new exhibits, and the interpretation of the grounds and memorials. George Washington's personal copy of his resignation speech of December 23, 1783, acquired by the Archives in 2007 and on display beneath the dome, is the centerpiece of this visitor experience, which I hope you will enjoy and find both memorable and moving.

Although the most significant national events transpired in the State House over two centuries ago, history is still being made within its walls today. Just this winter, in February 2020, statues of Harriet Tubman and Frederick Douglass were placed in the Old House of Delegates Chamber, where slavery was abolished in Maryland in November 1864. The inclusion of these self-liberated native Marylanders, who dedicated their lives to helping others attain freedom, is a step toward balancing the portrayal of our state's history in its most important public building.

In the introduction to his architectural study of the State House, written in 1971, then-State Archivist Morris L. Radoff said that "any building as old as the Maryland State House gathers around it, with the years, much legend and a great many half truths." Any Annapolitan would likely agree with his summation. But, as this book reveals, those legends, and the whole truth associated with them, together weave a monumental narrative befitting this landmark of Maryland and American history. It is a story that continues today, as the State House remains at the center of Maryland government and we meet the challenges of the twenty-first century.

Timothy D. Baker

Timothy D. Baker
State Archivist and
Commissioner of Land Patents

State House Floor Plan

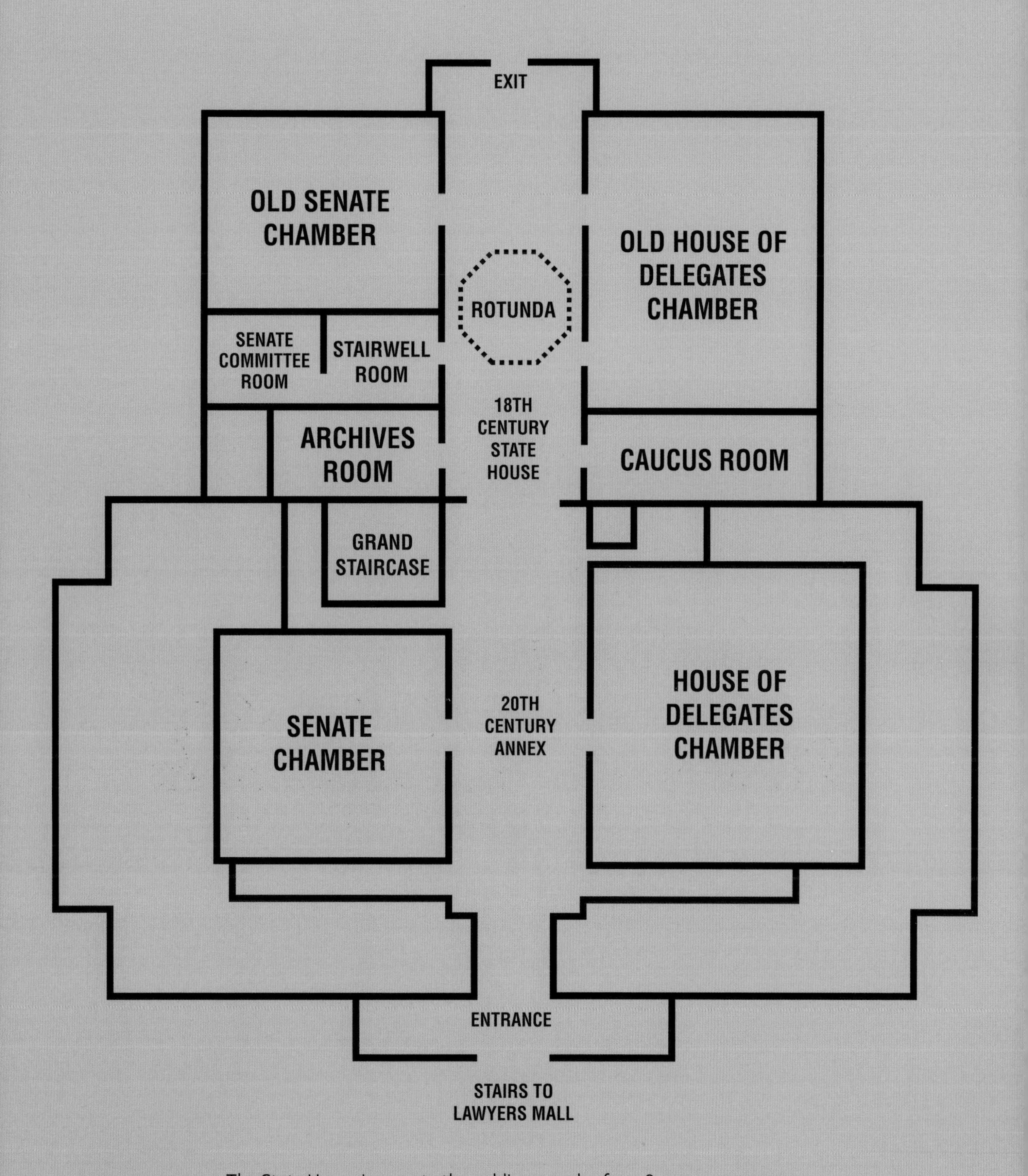

The State House is open to the public every day from 8:30 a.m.–5:00 p.m., except Christmas and New Year's Day. Visitors are required to show photo ID.

A Front View of the State House &c. at Annapolis the Capital of Maryland, attributed to Charles Willson Peale, 1789.

The Maryland State House

FROM 1769 TO TODAY

The Maryland State House is one of the most historic—and architecturally significant—state houses in the nation. Both houses of the legislature first used the State House in November 1779, making it the oldest state house still in continuous legislative use. This was ten years after the General Assembly, in December 1769, passed legislation that called for the building of "one good and Commodious House to be called the Stadt House."

This was actually the third State House built on this site, the highest point in the city. The first was built soon after the capital of the colony moved from St. Mary's City to Annapolis in 1695; it burned down in 1704. The second state house on the site was built by 1707 and was used for sixty years by the state government and the courts but, by 1769, was determined to be too small to accommodate the growing state government and in such poor condition that it would have to be replaced. The new building, as noted by the legislature, was to be "for the Holding Assemblies and Provincial Courts as for providing safe and secure Repositories for the Public Records."

Charles Wallace was named the "undertaker," or builder, of the new State House in June 1771, although the second State House was not demolished until December of that year. Joseph Horatio Anderson is credited as the original architect for this State House. Very little is known about Anderson, and the only other architectural project credited to him is Whitehall, a Georgian country house built in the 1760s by then Proprietary Governor Horatio Sharpe seven miles east of Annapolis. Whitehall is regarded as one of the finest Georgian houses in the country and is a National Historic Landmark.

The cornerstone for this new State House, which has never been found, was laid in March 1772. On April 2, the *Maryland Gazette* reported:

> *On Saturday last about Twelve o'Clock, his Excellency the Governor [Sir Robert Eden], attended by a Number of the principal Gentlemen of this City, was pleased to lay the First Stone of the Foundation of the State House; on which occasion a cold collation was provided for the Company, and after a few loyal and constitutional Toasts had circulated, the Gentlemen retired, the workmen giving Three Cheers on their Departure.*

The General Assembly of January 1777 appointed a committee to examine the State House to judge its completion and whether Mr. Wallace had complied with his contract. With the country then embroiled in the Revolutionary War, maintaining a sufficient workforce was a tremendous challenge, as Wallace explained in a letter to the General Assembly on December 28, 1779:

...when the British Fleet appeared in our Bay [in 1777] all my workmen left me and fled from the City to the interior parts of the State, where they got engaged in Business, and though I made every exertion in my Power, I could not thereafter draw together one fourth part of the sufficient Number of Workmen, this Event greatly retarded the Work, and occasioned my being under the necessity of paying very high Wages in 1779, for work which could, and would have been executed in 1777 for moderate terms.

The original dome on the State House was more aptly described as a cupola and was quickly determined to be insufficient for the size and grandeur of the building. In addition, the roof, almost flat and covered in metal, leaked from the earliest days of the completion of the building.

Proposals to increase the slant of the roof and cover it with wooden shingles, as well as to improve the dome were sought, and a contract was awarded to a local architect, Joseph Clark, about whom very little is known. It is possible that Clark drew his inspiration for the design of the new dome from images in books in the Annapolis store run by his brother, Stephen Clark. His final design has a striking resemblance to the dome of the Schlossturm, the tower that is part of the palace of Karl-Wilhelm in Karlsruhe, Germany, built in 1715. What is certain is that, for almost 250 years, the State House has stood at the center of Annapolis history, politics, and society.

During those 250 years, the State House has undergone many repairs, renovations, and restorations as well as the addition, and subsequent removal, of two nineteenth-century annexes. The present annex that houses the two modern legislative chambers has been in use since 1904. Despite the many changes over the centuries, the guardians of the Maryland State House have never lost the sense of the importance of the history that has taken place here.

Front Elevation of the State House [unbuilt], attributed to Joseph Horatio Anderson, ca. 1772.

State House before 1881.

In 1960, the State House was designated a National Historic Landmark, on the same day as Mount Vernon and Monticello. While there have been repeated attempts to return the Old Senate Chamber to its eighteenth-century appearance, the Old House of Delegates Chamber has been used in many different ways with little regard for its architectural or legislative history.

Over the centuries, the state of Maryland has conducted many campaigns of furnishings, repairs, and maintenance, but no major changes to the interior were made until 1858, when the House of Delegates Chamber was enlarged to accommodate a growing body of delegates. Gas lighting and steam heating were installed, and an annex to the building was constructed to house the State Library. The new library was entered by a grand staircase with the Great Seal of Maryland above. At the same time, a separate building was built on State Circle to house the office of the comptroller and the Land Office. A fireproof room for the safe storage of records within the State House, with a vaulted ceiling and a brick floor, was constructed and has been known since as the Archives Room.

In 1886, yet another annex was added to the building, this time a rectangular one with a passageway from the existing 1858 annex. The main purpose of this new space was to increase the size of the library.

By the turn of the twentieth century, it was determined that major changes to the State House were needed, including an entirely new annex. Not only was the rectangular annex very poorly built but the existing legislative chambers were too small for the work of the House and Senate. The Baltimore firm Baldwin & Pennington was engaged to carry out the needed changes. First, the two nineteenth-century additions were demolished and the new one that is still in use today was completed by 1904.

State House ca. 1890 showing second nineteenth-century annex.

This addition to the building, which is actually larger than the original eighteenth-century State House, houses both chambers of the legislature, as well as offices for the president of the Senate and the speaker of the House of Delegates. It also includes lounges for members behind each legislative chamber and, on the second floor, offices for the staff of the governor and lieutenant governor.

Once the new annex was completed, the commission in charge of the construction turned its attention to the condition of the eighteenth-century building. The findings were dire: "... portions of some of the beams which support the second floor are rotten." This was of such concern that the inaugural reception for the new governor, Edwin Warfield, was held in the Old Senate Chamber rather than on the second floor as had been the custom.

Aside from several restoration and re-creation projects in the Old Senate Chamber, and the two rooms that were created out of the Old House of Delegates Chamber, little significant work has taken place since the early years of the twentieth century. A new fire suppression system was installed in 2011 and electrical wiring, plumbing, and heating and air conditioning have been updated, but the building has remained very much the same as it appeared after the addition of the 1904 annex. Over the past decade, however, both historic chambers have been carefully examined and researched to discover and document their architectural and decorative histories, resulting in the restored chambers that are on view today.

As the historic chambers were being researched and restored, the Maryland State Archives commissioned a study, in 2007, of how to improve the interpretation and exhibits visitors see when they come to the State House. The State House Welcome Center had been closed since 2007, so people coming to the State House without a guide needed information about the building and its history. The study resulted in the Master Plan for the Maryland State House Visitor Experience, which laid out, in detail, how each area of the building and the grounds would be interpreted to explore four centuries of Maryland history.

Maryland's Art Collection

Just as historic as the building itself is the collection of paintings, sculpture, silver, and furniture on display throughout the State House. This collection dates from the earliest days of the occupation of the building when Charles Willson Peale's portrait of William Pitt was hung in the Old Senate Chamber in 1774. Soon after, another Peale painting, *Washington, Lafayette and Tilghman at Yorktown,* was installed in what is now the Old House of Delegates Chamber in 1784. In February 2020, two new works of art were placed in this chamber: bronze sculptures of Frederick Douglass and Harriet Tubman, both Maryland natives who played vital roles in the abolition movement of the nineteenth century.

As evidenced by the addition of these two works, the state-owned art collection continues to interpret historic events and people in American and Maryland history. Visitors to the State House can see such treasures as the USS *Maryland* silver service that dates to the early twentieth century and original furniture created by John Shaw for the State House in the late eighteenth century. Works from the state-owned art collection can also be seen throughout the state office complex in Annapolis. It is managed by the Maryland Commission on Artistic Property of the Maryland State Archives.

Portraits of noteworthy eighteenth-century men and women. Those on white background are known to have attended George Washington's resignation ceremony, Senate Committee Room.

"I wish'd to be the founder of a collection of Portraits,
which has the promise of becoming a rich and highly
Gallery of distinguished men..."
CHARLES WILLSON PEALE, JULY 1824
SIR ROBERT EDEN
DANIEL OF ST. THOMAS JENIFER
GEORGE PLATER
JEREMIAH TOWNLEY CHASE
WILLIAM SMALLWOOD
JOHN HOSKINS STONE
WILLIAM PACA
JAMES McHENRY
OTHO HOLLAND WILLIAMS
JOSHUA BARNEY
HEROES OF THE REVOLUTION
WITNESSES TO THE RESIGNATION
REVOLUTIONARY LEADERS

STATE HOUSE
OLD SENATE CHAMBER
STAIRWELL ROOM
OLD HOUSE OF DELEGATES CHAMBER

The 18th-Century State House

THE ROTUNDA & DOME

At the center of the eighteenth-century State House is the rotunda, beneath the interior of the dome that still retains some of its original eighteenth-century plasterwork. For many years, the rotunda was entered through a small pedimented portico that was part of Joseph Anderson's original design. In 1882–83, when substantial improvements were also made to the grounds, a larger portico decorated with Corinthian columns replaced the smaller one. Until the construction of the twentieth-century annex, this was the main public entrance to the State House.

During the first half of the nineteenth century, no substantial structural work was performed. Projects that were undertaken, mostly around 1858, included the installation of steam heat and gas lighting, enlarging the House of Delegates Chamber to accommodate a growing number of delegates, and constructing an annex to the building for the State Library. A separate building on the grounds to provide offices for the comptroller and the Land Office was also constructed.

Even with the improvements, by the 1870s, a century after the State House was completed, the building had fallen into disrepair. Of great concern was the condition of the floors, especially the second floor that was sagging badly. The collapse of a floor in the Virginia state capitol in 1870, killing sixty-two people and injuring hundreds more, made the issue even more urgent.

In 1876, the legislature appropriated funds for a major renovation that included work to reinforce the support of the second floor as well as the dome, the digging of a new cellar, repairs to the roof, and other renovations. The extent of the work and the condition of the building resulted in the project costing three-and-a-half times the original appropriation. It was during this campaign that both the Old Senate and the Old House of Delegates Chambers were decorated in highly ornate Victorian style.

The Rotunda

The rotunda of today appears much as it has since 1881 when the black and white marble tile floors and columns were installed. One change has been the removal of the spitoons which graced its marble floors during the early twentieth century. Above four of the doors are historic portraits of the first four Lords Baltimore, on loan from the Enoch Pratt Free Library: George, Cecil, Charles, and Benedict Leonard Calvert.

Under the dome stands a case displaying George Washington's personal copy of the speech he gave in the Old Senate Chamber on December 23, 1783 resigning his commission as commander-in-chief of the Continental Army. Considered by historians to be one of the most important milestones in American history, Washington's resignation from power set the important precedent of the military being under civilian authority and the president of the United States being the commander-in-chief.

The evening before he submitted his resignation, Congress held a public dinner and dance for George Washington, which was attended by some 200 guests. Thirteen toasts were offered and, in response, Washington offered his own: "Competent Powers to Congress for general Purposes," an expression of his oft-stated belief that Congress should be given more authority. Following the dinner and toasts, a gala dance was held in the rotunda and, according to contemporary accounts, Washington danced with every lady present.

Schlossturm tower in Karlsruhe, Germany.

The Dome

When the Confederation Congress came to Annapolis to meet in the Old Senate Chamber from November 1783 to August 1784, they found a State House that was still unfinished. Although the Senate Chamber was complete, the building's roof was not and it had leaked during the last few winters, damaging the upstairs rooms. The roof was almost flat and was originally sheathed with copper that blew off in a storm in 1775. The dome, or cupola, atop the State House was variously described as inadequate, unimpressive, and too small for the building. It also leaked.

A survey of the timbers in the dome in 1784 revealed that they were so decayed by water damage that a new dome would be required. In the opinion of a local official, Intendant of Revenue Daniel of St. Thomas Jenifer:

> *It was originally constructed contrary to all rules of architecture; it ought to have been built double instead of single, and a staircase between the two domes, leading up to the lanthorn. The water should have been carried off by eaves, instead of being drawn to the center of the building, to two small conductors, which are liable to be choked by ice, and overflowed by rains. That it was next to impossible, under present construction, that it could have been made right.*

By February 1785, Jenifer had engaged Joseph Clark, an Annapolis architect and builder, to repair the roof and the dome. Clark first raised the pitch of the roof to facilitate the runoff of water and covered it with cypress shingles. The crowning achievement of Clark's work on the State House was, of course, the extraordinary dome that he designed and built. The source of Clark's inspiration for the unusual design of the dome is not known, but it is very similar to one in Karlsruhe, Germany called the Schlossturm:

> *The Annapolis dome is in its proportions like the original Karlsruhe tower. Possibly its more classical feeling is a result of the universal trend of architectural styles rather than the influence of the altered Schlossturm. Yet the arched windows below the architrave in Annapolis, one with the lower part closed, are like the windows below the architrave in Karlsruhe in all of which the lower parts are closed. The horizontal oval windows below the main curving section of the dome in Annapolis resemble the vertical ovals in the equivalent part of the Karlsruhe tower. The small square windows above the balustrade in Annapolis are almost identical with those below the architrave in Karlsruhe. And the balustrades and the architraves themselves in both buildings are similarly placed.**

Watching and Waiting, Annapolis in the War of 1812, by Richard Schlect, 2012.

*Winifred and Douglas Gordon. "The Dome of the Annapolis State House." *Maryland Historical Magazine*, Vol. 67, No. 3, Fall 1972.

Interior of dome showing framing details and names left by workers over the centuries.

By the summer of 1788, the exterior of the new dome was complete. It was constructed of timber and no metal nails were used in its construction and, to this day, it is held together by wooden pegs reinforced by iron straps forged by an Annapolis ironmonger. The beams are of cypress from the Eastern Shore of Maryland. Although the exterior of the dome was completed by 1788, the interior was not completed until 1797.

By 1794, Joseph Clark's participation in the project was finished. He had found the work frustrating from the beginning because of difficulty in obtaining needed materials and a constant lack of funds. His departure left it to John Shaw, the noted Annapolis cabinet-maker, to oversee completion, which took another three years. Shaw was a central figure in the maintenance and furnishing of the State House almost until his death in 1829.

Over the years, the dome has been maintained, painted, and repaired by workers from Annapolis, many of whom have, literally, left their mark on the interior of the dome. On many of the enormous beams that make up the structure of the dome are the names of these men, some dating from the eighteenth century. The dome has also been an important lookout in times of trouble, especially during the War of 1812.

In the early twentieth century, a commission charged with overseeing the construction of the new annex and Court of Appeals building recommended that the dome be replaced with a new, steel dome of the same proportions as this one. The General Assembly thought the better of it and appropriated funds for the repair and restoration of the eighteenth-century dome.

Newly gilded and copper-sheathed acorn on dome, 1996.

Interior of dome showing inner and outer structures.

Cutaway drawing of dome, Historic American Buildings Survey, 1986.

The Acorn

To anchor the lightning rod atop the dome, Clark placed an acorn-shaped wooden finial, which he covered in copper and gold. The acorn is a traditional symbol of strength and potential. This acorn survived, and did its job of securing the lightning rod, for more than 225 years. In 1996, an examination of the dome and the acorn revealed that almost all of the material in the acorn, its pedestal, and the lightning rod was original from the eighteenth century. The acorn was found to have been made of bald cedar and sheathed in copper sheets secured with nails. In addition, the original paint scheme had survived under many layers of paint revealing that the lower part of acorn had been green and the top was gilt. Because the copper sheathing had failed to keep the water out, the entire structure was rotting and considered to be in danger of collapse in the next heavy wind storm.

During the summer and fall of 1996, the original acorn, which weighed an estimated 800 pounds, and its pedestal were removed by helicopter. A new acorn was constructed by thirty-two Maryland artisans who each volunteered to create one layer of cypress, called "wheels," for the new acorn. It is clad in copper and gilded on the top, as was the original. The lightning rod remains intact and continues to serve as it has since the 1790s, although a steel sleeve has been placed around it inside the new acorn to strengthen it. The acorn was regilded in 2011.

In 2010, it was determined that the dome was badly in need of maintenance, especially the removal of existing paint layers and repainting, repairs to the balustrades, reglazing and painting of the windows, and other work. Advanced microscopy techniques were used to investigate the paint still on the dome, as well as the history of its other features. At least twenty-three layers of paint were found and the cypress shingles on the "drum" of the dome were determined to date from the 1780s. Every nail was handmade by a blacksmith, and the windows were original. The results of the investigation indicated an amazing level of durability for the structure and its paint.

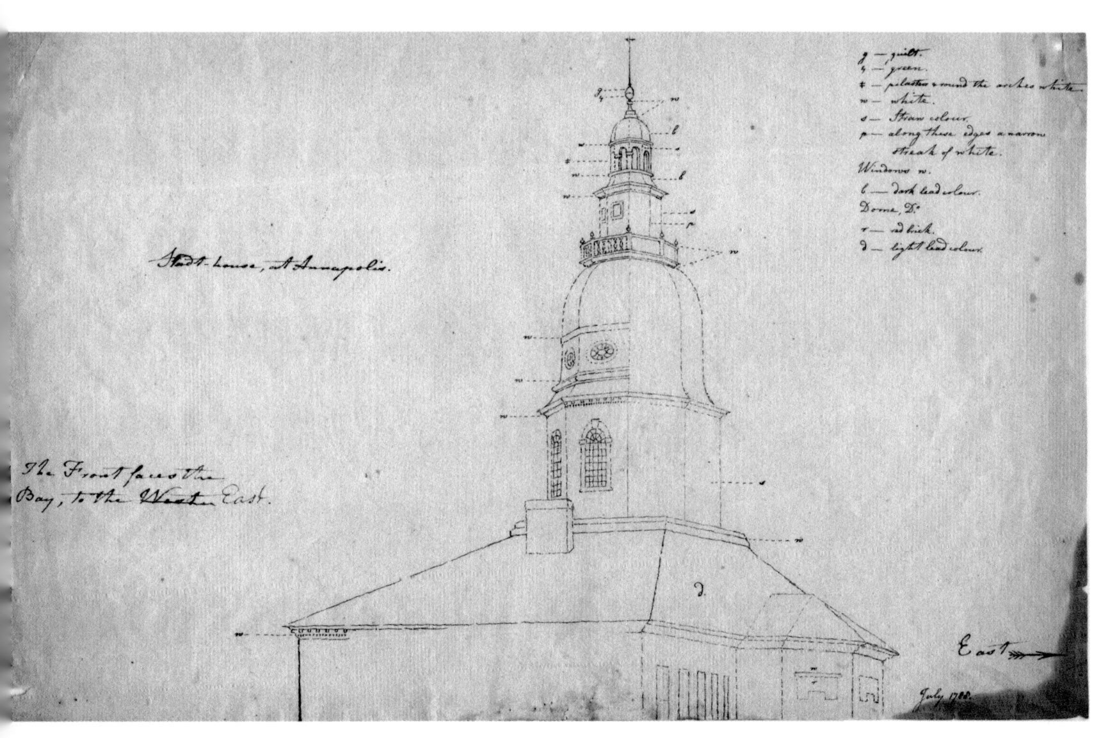

State House drawing, noting original colors, by Charles Willson Peale, 1788.

At the time, there was discussion about returning the dome to its original bright colors as documented by Charles Willson Peale, as well as contemporary press accounts. Research by the Maryland Historical Trust and the Maryland State Archives was not able to determine exactly when the present white was introduced but it is believed to date from the 1820s or 1830s. The decision to retain the use of white paint was based, in part, on the US Department of the Interior's Standards for Treatment of Historic Properties.

The Lightning Rod

The lighting rod that tops the dome is a "Franklin" rod, constructed and grounded according to Benjamin Franklin's specifications. At the time, the use of this type of lightning rod could also be seen as a political statement by showing support for Franklin's theories on protection of public buildings from lightning strikes and, thereby, rejecting an opposing theory supported by King George III in favor of a rounded top of the rod. The pointed lightning rod atop such an important new public building was a powerful symbol of the independence and ingenuity of the young nation.

As an architect trained in London, and with a brother who had a bookshop in Annapolis, Clark would have been familiar with the writings of Benjamin Franklin. In addition, the artist Charles Willson Peale confirmed Clark's design. On July 14, 1788, Peale and one of his brothers went to Philadelphia to see Franklin to ask his opinion on the efficacy of a lightning rod on the State House. They were unable to see Franklin, but did consult with Robert Patterson and David Rittenhouse, both eminent authorities on the physical sciences. Peale reported that Mr. Rittenhouse was of the opinion that:

> *. . . if the points are good and near enough the Building and the part going into the ground so deep as to get into soft earth no danger is to be apprehended, but if the end could be put in water of a Well it would be best.*

Benjamin Franklin (1706–1790), by Jean-Jacques Caffieri, 1775–85.

State House dome fire suppression system being tested.

The engineering of the lightning rod and the acorn, which holds it in place, represents an astonishing achievement. It was built by local blacksmith, Simon Retallick. Rising 28 feet into the air, the rod is anchored to the top of the dome. It then runs through a pedestal and the acorn and is surmounted by a copper weathervane; it also serves as a flagpole for the American and Maryland flags. The acorn and pedestal have served to stabilize the Franklin rod and hold it in place for more than two centuries of the extremes of Maryland weather. The Franklin rod has proved its value a number of times over the years, most recently in July 2016 when a bolt of lightning struck the dome activating a deluge system that was installed in 1999.

The dome that Clark designed and built for the State House has been the defining landmark of the Annapolis skyline for more than 225 years. It was also, for many years, a popular spot from which to observe the city and the Chesapeake Bay beyond. Charles Willson Peale planned a dramatic cyclorama of Annapolis with eight views from the dome and a centerpiece drawing of State Circle from Cornhill Street. Only the drawing of the State House was completed and published in the *Columbian Magazine* in 1789. Thomas Jefferson and James Madison spent a most enjoyable three hours in September 1790 on the balcony of the dome with his friend, Thomas Lee Shippen, and a local doctor, John Shaaff, who entertained them by "opening the roofs of the houses and telling us the history of each family who lived in them."

The dome is now closed to the public for reasons of safety and preservation, but it remains the most visible symbol of the history of the state and the extraordinary history of the building it adorns.

Left:
George Calvert, First Lord Baltimore (1579–1632), by Daniel Mytens the Elder, ca. 1630.

Middle:
Cecilius (Cecil) Calvert, Second Lord Baltimore (1605–1675) by Gerard Soest, ca. 1670.

Right:
Charles Calvert, Third Lord Baltimore (1637–1714/15), by Sir Godfrey Kneller, ca. 1690.

The Calverts: The Proprietary Lords Baltimore of Maryland

The full-length portraits of the Lords Baltimore portray an entire dynasty of colonial proprietors, the Barons (or Lords) of Baltimore. The proprietary rule of the Lords Baltimore ended with the American Revolution in 1776. These pictures, on loan from the Enoch Pratt Free Library in Baltimore, bring to life the earliest history of our state.

George Calvert, First Lord Baltimore

George Calvert was born at Kiplin Hall in Yorkshire, England in 1579. He served as secretary of state for King James I, but, after revealing his Catholic faith, he had to leave his service to the crown. At his request, the king granted him land in Newfoundland, Canada where Calvert and his family established the colony of Avalon. George Calvert was also given the title of Baron of Baltimore. However, the long, brutal winter of 1628–29 prompted Calvert to return to England and plead for a grant of land in the mid-Atlantic, north of the Potomac River, where he could grow tobacco. The new king, Charles I, granted the Charter of Maryland to Cecil Calvert in June 1632, shortly after George's death in April of that year.

Cecilius (Cecil) Calvert, Second Lord Baltimore

Cecil Calvert succeeded to the title of Lord Baltimore upon the death of his father, George, and was the one to whom the Charter of Maryland was actually granted by King Charles I in 1632. He never traveled to Maryland and he was an active promoter of religious tolerance. The portrait includes his grandson, Charles, who died in 1680. Cecil is shown holding a map of the colony of Maryland, and a young enslaved attendant in the portrait attests to Calvert's wealth. Although his identity is unknown, the child's clothing indicates his status as a household servant.

Charles Calvert, Third Lord Baltimore

Charles Calvert was the first of the proprietors to reside in Maryland. Born in England in 1637, he came to Maryland in 1661 at age twenty-four. He continued his father's policy of religious toleration, along with his family's Catholic faith. He struggled with William Penn over the northern boundary of Maryland, leading to his return to England in 1684. In 1689, during the Glorious Revolution in England, the proprietorship of Maryland was returned to the crown because of Calvert's continued allegiance to the Roman Catholic church.

Left:
Benedict Leonard Calvert, Fourth Lord Baltimore (1679–1715), Artist unknown, ca. 1715.

Middle:
Charles Calvert, Fifth Lord Baltimore (1699–1751), by Allan Ramsay, ca. 1740.

Right:
Frederick Calvert, Sixth Lord Baltimore (1731/2–1771), by Johann Ludwig Tietz, ca. 1750.

Below:
Crest of the Lords Baltimore.

Benedict Leonard Calvert, Fourth Lord Baltimore

The first of the Lords Baltimore to be born in Maryland, Benedict Leonard Calvert converted to Anglicanism in 1713. Upon learning of his son's conversion, Charles Calvert, Third Lord Baltimore, cut off his son's income, making him dependent upon Queen Anne, whom he petitioned for support. Immediately upon Benedict Leonard's death, the title passed to his eldest son, Charles Calvert, and Maryland was returned to the Calverts as a proprietary colony.

Charles Calvert, Fifth Lord Baltimore

With his father's sudden death, Charles Calvert inherited the title of Lord Baltimore at only sixteen years of age. In 1721, having reached the age of majority, he assumed control of the colony. In 1732, he became the first of the proprietors to visit Maryland in nearly fifty years to look after his interests in a boundary dispute with William Penn's sons. A lawsuit by the Penns dragged on until 1750 when the lord chief justice decided in favor of the Penns. Under this decision, the Mason and Dixon line was established in 1769 as the boundary between Maryland and Pennsylvania. Charles died in England at the age of fifty-one.

Frederick Calvert, Sixth Lord Baltimore

As the only legitimate son of Charles Calvert, Fifth Lord Baltimore, Frederick succeeded to the proprietorship of Maryland in 1751 at the age of twenty. He had little interest in administering his duties and never visited Maryland. He died in Naples, Italy in 1771 and, in his will, left all of his estates, including the Province of Maryland, to his illegitimate son Henry Harford. Frederick's sisters, Louisa and Caroline, contested the will. The Revolutionary War delayed the settlement until 1780 when an act of Parliament provided for the sisters. Caroline was the wife of Sir Robert Eden, Maryland's last proprietary governor and the first Baronet of Maryland.

WILLIAM PITT:
"THE GREAT COMMONER"

The Old Senate Chamber

This chamber is one of the most historic spaces in American history. As it appears today, it is a deeply-researched restoration to what the room would have looked like on December 23, 1783. This date is important as it was when a bedrock of American history and government was born: the military of this new nation would always be under the command of the civilian authority.

From November 26, 1783 until August 13, 1784, the Congress of the Confederation met in this room to conduct some of the most historic and important business of the new nation. Most significantly, on December 23, General George Washington came before Congress to resign his commission as commander-in-chief of the Continental Army. Victory had been won at Yorktown more than two years earlier, but there was great uncertainty as to how the government and the military would function in the new nation. Many thought that Washington would become its unelected leader, almost by default, as there was no obvious person to assume the role.

This historic event was attended by many of the most influential people in Maryland and the nation, some of whose portraits are on display in the Senate Committee Room. Also in attendance were the city's most prominent women who could only watch from the "ladies' balcony" because women were not allowed on the floor of the Senate Chamber. In the gallery is a statue of Mary "Molly" Ridout, who watched the ceremony from the crowded balcony. She wrote one of the very few first-hand accounts of the ceremony in a letter to her mother in England, noting that "... many tears were shed."

Old Senate Chamber with statue of George Washington and portrait of William Pitt.

Old Senate Chamber with statue of Molly Ridout in balcony.

Also in the room for this historic event was the portrait of William Pitt by one of the most celebrated artists of the day, Charles Willson Peale. Pitt, a member of the British Parliament and former prime minister, was revered in the American colonies for his strong opposition to the Stamp Act.

On January 14, 1784, two weeks after Washington's resignation, Congress ratified the Treaty of Paris, which officially ended the Revolutionary War and made America an independent nation. From that day until August of that year, Annapolis was the capital of the new nation. Another milestone was the appointment of Thomas Jefferson as minister plenipotentiary for negotiating treaties of amity and commerce with the nations of Europe on May 7, 1784.

Why did Congress convene in Annapolis in the first place? Because there was no permanent capital, by June 1783 Congress was seeking a permanent seat of government. It had moved from Philadelphia to nearby Princeton to avoid the riotous troops seeking payment for their service in the Revolutionary War. Maryland had hoped to make Annapolis the nation's new capital and what better place than the newly constructed State House? To accommodate Congress, the state offered the use of the Senate Chamber, the finest room in the new State House, as well as the governor's mansion, Jennings House, for the use of the president of Congress.

In recognition of the historic events that took place here, the Maryland State House was designated a National Historic Landmark in 1960. Washington's resignation has been memorialized in three nineteenth-century paintings: *General George Washington Resigning His Commission* by John Trumbull, which hangs in the rotunda of the US Capitol; *George Washington Surrendering His Commission* by Francis Blackwell Mayer, in the Mint Museum in Charlotte, North Carolina; and *Washington Resigning His Commission* by Edwin White, which can be seen in the grand stairwell of the State House. It is also the moment depicted atop Baltimore's Washington Monument where Washington is seen facing Annapolis with his arm outstretched, offering his scrolled commission. All three paintings provide evidence of the appearance of the chamber when Washington resigned in 1783.

Early History of the Senate Chamber

The members of the Maryland Senate first convened in the chamber on November 8, 1779 and continued to meet there for every legislative session until 1904. In 1780, accommodations for fifteen senators, including the president, and at least one clerk, a messenger, and a doorkeeper were required. The room's focal points, the president's niche and dais at the front and the visitors' gallery at the rear, both contained rich classical details that reflected designs published in architectural design books of the time. The fireplace wall featured a false door that mirrored the entrance door to the adjoining Senate Committee Room, an element of the Georgian design of the chamber that called for symmetry in all four elevations.

Old Senate Chamber niche and dais as restored, 2015.

The niche was a raised space for the Senate president, symbolizing the power of his position. It was framed by engaged Ionic columns supporting a classical pediment. The floor plan of the State House published in the *Columbian Magazine* in February 1789 is the earliest known document showing the galleries supported by four columns.

Although progress was slowed by the Revolutionary War, evidence suggests that no expense was spared in its construction, especially in the Senate Chamber. Numerous first-hand accounts from the eighteenth century describe the splendor of the new State House and the Senate Chamber. Hugh Williamson, delegate to Congress from North Carolina, wrote that "The State House here is certainly an elegant Building. The Room we are to sit in is perhaps the prettyest in America." David Howell of Rhode Island said, "The State House & the House assigned for the President [Jennings House] are spacious & elegantly finished, far exceeding those buildings in Philadelphia."

Old Senate Chamber renovation, by George Frederick, ca. 1886.

Desecration of the Sacred Space

By the last quarter of the nineteenth century, the State House and its legislative chambers were showing signs of wear and almost everything needed to be repaired or replaced. There were concerns that the floor of the room above the Senate Chamber might collapse, as had happened in the Virginia capitol in 1870. The General Assembly not only wanted repairs to be made throughout the State House, it also wanted finally to have a modern heating system installed.

In 1876, a Baltimore architect, George A. Frederick, was hired to supervise renovations to the building. However, while Frederick's original intent was to preserve the Senate Chamber and other historic rooms, everything was in such disrepair that the actual cost of the project grew to more than three-and-a-half times his original estimate.

The result of Frederick's renovations was an elaborate Victorian room that completely obliterated any hint of its eighteenth-century architectural heritage. The niche and windows were covered with heavy drapery, and the ceiling was divided in two with a heavy beam installed to secure the floor of the room above. The public gallery and original doors, including the false door on the north wall, were removed. The only acknowledgement of the historic events of 1783–84 was White's *Washington Resigning His Commission* which hung on the wall where the fireplace had been. These actions, regarded by the public as a desecration of an historic space, caused widespread outrage.

Amid the destruction of the eighteenth-century chamber, a few important features were saved. Two of the original columns from the gallery were saved by twelve-year-old Daniel R. Randall, a descendant of John Randall, who is believed to have worked on the State House in the eighteenth century. According to family legend, Daniel purchased them with his own wages from his work in the building. The niche, with its wood pilasters and plaster arch, was not destroyed but merely covered over with drapes, thus retaining a piece of the original architecture, as well as all-important evidence of the original paint.

The 1905 Restoration

With the completion of the new annex from 1902–04 and the convening of both houses of the General Assembly in their new chambers, it was finally time to undo the damage of the 1870s by restoring the Old Senate Chamber to its appearance when Congress met in Annapolis.

Old Senate Chamber after restoration, by John Appleton Wilson, 1905.

Governor Edwin Warfield appointed a sub-committee of the existing State House Building Commission to restore the Old Senate Chamber to how it appeared on December 23, 1783. Two of the most prominent members of the committee were John Appleton Wilson, who had worked on the 1894 restoration attempt, and Josias Pennington, the principal architect of the new annex. Other members came from a number of patriotic societies.

Wilson contacted George Frederick in hopes of securing his detailed measured drawings of the chamber before the 1876 work. Frederick refused, saying he had packed up his papers and was leaving the city. Without the aid of Frederick's drawings, which have never been found, Wilson was forced to consult other state records and documents, eighteenth-century fragments from the chamber, and the existing architectural elements to complete his restoration. Highlights of Wilson's restoration included a new ceiling, with the heavy support beam of 1876 removed, a new floor, a three-step dais, a rebuilt gallery, a new chimney and fireplace, and bench seating below the windows. The original columns from the gallery that had been salvaged by Daniel Randall were returned, enabling Wilson to re-create the exact height of the gallery.

The room was replastered and painted a "colonial green," based on John Trumbull's painting *Washington Resigning His Commission*, and original plaster fragments were found in the president's niche. To complete the restored chamber as a shrine to George Washington, the state's historic painting of *Washington, Lafayette and Tilghman at Yorktown* by Charles Willson Peale was installed above the fireplace. Although this restoration was considered accurate by the standards of the day, it was a Colonial Revival restoration based more on conjecture than supporting evidence. Many of Wilson's "errors" would not be corrected until the most recent restoration.

On June 1, 1936, Governor Harry Nice formed a commission to restore the Old Senate Chamber. After much debate, it decided that the furnishing of the Old Senate Chamber would reflect the chamber's appearance during regular use by the Maryland Senate in the late eighteenth century, rather than specifically when in use by Congress.

Desk, Senate (reproduction), by Enrico Liberti, 1940.

Enrico Liberti, who had immigrated from Italy in 1920, was a cabinet-maker who operated the Chimney Corner Shop in Baltimore. He was commissioned to make reproductions of John Shaw's 1797 desks and chairs that may have been part of the original furnishings of the Senate Chamber. Liberti made fourteen desks and twenty-three chairs for display. To complete the furnishings, the Maryland Society of Colonial Dames acquired the original Senate president's desk and chair made by the shop of John Shaw in 1797. This restoration was completed in 1942.

The 200th anniversary of Washington's resignation and the ratification of the Treaty of Paris were celebrated by the state in 1983 and 1984 with parades and a reenactment of the resignation ceremony. For this anniversary, the Society of Senates Past commissioned a figure of George Washington wearing an exact replica of the uniform he wore that day that is now in the National Museum of American History of the Smithsonian Institution. The head of Washington was modeled on the bust made from life by French sculptor Jean-Antoine Houdon in 1785 at Mount Vernon. This figure was on display for thirty years.

Restoration of the Old Senate Chamber 2006–2015

By 2000, the plaster in the chamber was beginning to fail and new paint was already peeling. Attempts to find the cause of these issues and to address them went on for several years. An investigation determined that the plaster used in Wilson's 1905 restoration was of a poor quality and that approximately twenty layers of incompatible paints trapped large quantities of moisture in the walls. It was soon determined that all of the plaster in the room needed to be removed, exposing even more, previously unknown, architectural elements. For the next three years, the Maryland Historical Trust and the Maryland State Archives worked with consultants to conduct an "above-ground archaeological" study of the chamber.

Armchair, Senate (reproduction), by Enrico Liberti, 1940.

In 2009, the State House Trust convened the Old Senate Chamber Architectural Advisory Committee. This committee was charged with determining whether sufficient physical and documentary evidence existed to warrant undertaking a new restoration of the chamber that was more credible and accurate than the 1905 and 1940 iterations. Essentially, could a more accurate restoration be achieved with the new information now available? After an exhaustive review, the committee determined that, indeed, a more accurate restoration of the chamber was possible thanks to new technologies and the discovery of new architectural and archival evidence. The committee's recommendation was accepted by the State House Trust and, in September 2012, the architectural firm of Mesick Cohen Wilson Baker was awarded the contract to lead the restoration of the chamber.

The architects were to reproduce the Old Senate Chamber as it existed when George Washington stood before Congress to resign his commission at noon on December 23, 1783. Every effort was made to ensure the authenticity of the room as it appeared during that ceremony. Unless substantial evidence, both architectural and archival, existed for the inclusion of an element, it would not be included. However, some of the final design elements in the chimneypiece and door treatments had to be based on some level of conjecture. In these instances, decisions were made using examples in comparably-dated local houses, most notably the Chase-Lloyd House a block away on Maryland Avenue.

Several key changes were made in the 2015 restoration from previous efforts. The original color of the room was discovered, the window seats were removed, a new floor was installed, and the height of the south doorway leading to the rotunda was altered. Perhaps the most visible aspect of the 2015 restoration is the absence of a chandelier. Although there were strong arguments for including a chandelier, a more conservative approach was taken due to the lack of specific evidence as to the presence or absence of lighting fixtures in the chamber in 1783.

Old Senate Chamber before restoration, 2007.

Some of the biggest questions facing the committee related to the design of the gallery: were the ends of the original gallery concave or convex; why did the gallery terminate so awkwardly in the window wall; was it because the gallery was a change order or did Wilson get it wrong in the 1905 restoration and the ends should have turned inwards; are the columns on the outer ends really original; and what did the original ornamental plaster really look like?

To answer these questions, the gallery constructed in 1905 was carefully removed. This gave the architectural team access to the previously hidden walls and joist pockets. The removal uncovered an angled beam pocket in the east wall, which left no doubt that the rounded ends of the gallery had been convex.

Old Senate Chamber niche with exposed paint layers, 2014.

The restoration team spent a lot of time studying the niche, the only original architectural element of the chamber that was preserved during the renovation of 1876. One of the fascinating elements of the most recent study of the niche was the analysis of the various paint finishes. The discovery of matching layers of paint behind the wainscot on the fireplace side of the room and in the niche confirmed the original color of the room to be a fully-saturated yellow ochre distemper paint.

The newly-restored dais was returned to its eighteenth-century configuration based on architectural ghosting, nailing blocks, and the plan in the *Columbian Magazine* of 1789. The dais is now wider and only has two steps. The new Ionic columns were derived from architectural pattern books and match those at the Chase-Lloyd House.

Two architectural elements in the Old Senate Chamber that could not be accurately restored to their original appearance were the ceiling and the windows. The eighteenth-century ceiling was slightly higher than the one in the room today. Physical and archival evidence determined the exact height and width of the eighteenth-century window trim and sills; however, these could not be restored accurately without significant alterations to the window wall. The reconstructed two-tier shutters are fixed into place, as they were until 1818 when John Shaw added hinges and "backshutters."

Congressional Ceremonial Protocol

What furnishings were in the room at the time of the resignation ceremony in December 1783 and how were they arranged? Where did Washington stand to deliver his address? These were important questions as to how the space would be interpreted.

To answer these questions, every ceremony conducted by Congress between 1778 and 1783 was studied in the hopes of putting together the puzzle of recreating what might have happened on that day. For every new ceremony hosted by Congress, a new script was created that directed when members and visitors were meant to sit, stand, bow, and take off their hats, all highly symbolic gestures that were important aspects of politics in European courts. The nineteen side chairs and two armchairs in the chamber today are arranged in a semicircle based on the ceremonial protocol from a previous public audience before Congress.

According to the protocol established, the president and Congress were seated and covered (with hats on) when the secretary of Congress, Charles Thomson and two aides conducted Washington to his seat. After President Thomas Mifflin welcomed him, Washington arose to address Congress. When he finished his speech, Washington handed his commission to Mifflin.

The bronze statue of George Washington is placed where it is believed he stood to deliver his address to Congress. Washington is depicted in the emotional moment when he was compelled to steady his hands. James McHenry noted in a letter describing the ceremony that when "he spoke of the officers who had composed his family… he was obliged to support the paper with both hands."

The statue of Molly Ridout is in the gallery where she and other prominent Annapolis women witnessed the ceremony. Ridout authored one of the only contemporary accounts of the resignation ceremony and the only description left by a private citizen. The model for this statue was one of her direct descendants, Rachel Ridout.

The portrait of William Pitt by Charles Willson Peale was displayed above the mantel in the Senate Chamber until 1834. The portrait is in an allegorical setting filled with republican symbols. A more period-appropriate frame was produced for it to be displayed in the restored chamber.

George Washington and *Mary (Molly) Ridout,* by StudioEIS, 2014.

William Pitt (1708–1778)

By Charles Willson Peale, 1768

Known as "The Great Commoner" for his long-standing refusal to accept a title, William Pitt became a member of the House of Commons in 1735. In 1766, he finally accepted the title of Earl of Chatham and joined the House of Lords where he served as prime minister and Lord Privy Seal from July 1766–October 1768. He was an active supporter of colonial rights, and American colonists admired him for his opposition to the Stamp Act of 1765, in which Parliament taxed nearly every paper document passing through colonists' hands, including newspapers, licenses, and even playing cards. Pitt believed that Parliament should pursue increased trade with colonists, not taxation, to generate revenue.

William Pitt, 1st Earl of Chatham, by Joseph Wilton, 1766 or after.

While studying in London with artist Benjamin West, Charles Willson Peale was commissioned by a group of Virginia gentlemen to paint a portrait of Pitt. Peale made two full-length versions of the portrait, basing his likeness on a bust of Pitt by British sculptor Joseph Wilton. On returning to America, Peale heard that the Maryland legislature had commissioned a statue of Pitt for the State House and offered one of his two portraits to the state instead. The one that hangs in the Maryland State House was the first of the two versions Peale painted. The second is in the Westmoreland County Museum in Montross, Virginia.

Peale's portrait of Pitt depicts him with objects that carried particular meaning. He is shown in classical dress, which associated the statesman with Roman heroes who would have worn similar attire. It also avoided connecting Pitt with the English aristocracy, which might not have been received well by American viewers. He holds a copy of the Magna Carta in his left hand.

Other symbols in the portrait include an American Indian who, with a dog at his side, shows the faithfulness and firmness of America. There is an altar with a perpetual flame, illustrating the sacred cause of liberty, on which are carved busts of the famous Whigs, John Hampden and Algernon Sidney. In the background is the Banqueting House of Whitehall from which King Charles I was led to his execution in 1649.

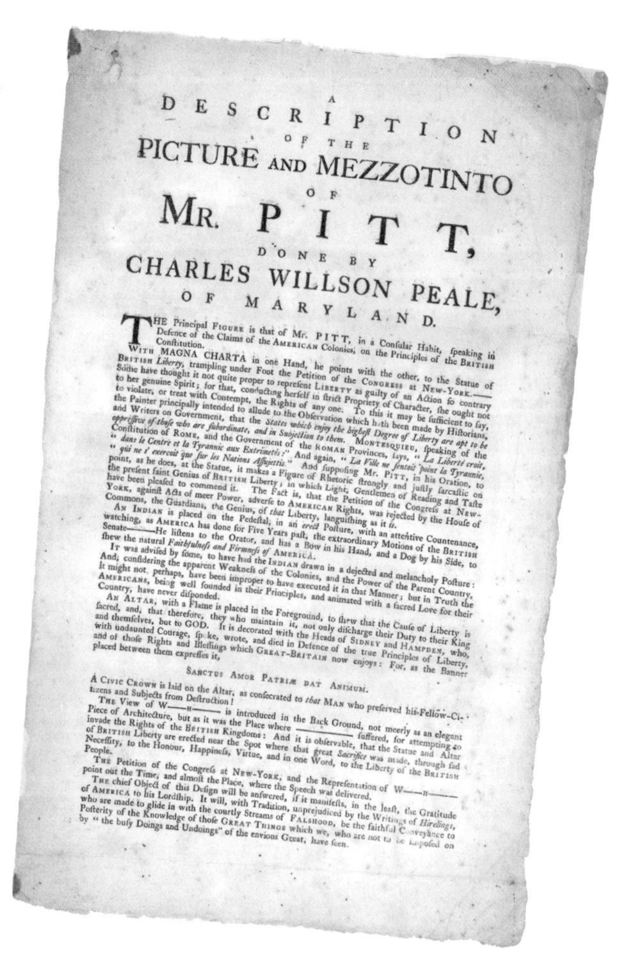

A DESCRIPTION OF THE PICTURE AND MEZZOTINTO OF MR. PITT, DONE BY CHARLES WILLSON PEALE, OF MARYLAND.

THE Principal FIGURE is that of Mr. PITT, in a Consular Habit, speaking in Defence of the Claims of the AMERICAN Colonies, on the Principles of the BRITISH Constitution.

WITH MAGNA CHARTA in one Hand, he points with the other, to the Statue of BRITISH *Liberty*, trampling under Foot the Petition of the CONGRESS at NEW-YORK.——Some have thought it not quite proper to represent LIBERTY as guilty of an Action so contrary to her genuine Spirit; for that, conducting herself in strict Propriety of Character, she ought not to violate, or treat with Contempt, the Rights of any one. To this it may be sufficient to say, the Painter principally intended to allude to the Observation which hath been made by Historians, and Writers on Government, that the *States which enjoy the highest Degree of Liberty are apt to be oppressive of those who are subordinate, and in Subjection to them.* MONTESQUIEU, speaking of the Constitution of ROME, and the Government of the ROMAN Provinces, says, "*La Liberté croit, dans le Centre et la Tyrannie aux Extrimetés:*" And again, "*La Ville ne sentoit point la Tyrannie, qui ne s'exercoit que sur les Nations Assujettis.*" And supposing Mr. PITT, in his Oration, to point, as he does, at the Statue, it makes a Figure of Rhetoric strongly and justly sarcastic on the present faint Genius of BRITISH Liberty; in which Light, Gentlemen of Reading and Taste have been pleased to commend it. The Fact is, that the Petition of the Congress at NEW-YORK, against Acts of meer Power, adverse to AMERICAN Rights, was rejected by the House of Commons, the Guardians, the Genius, of *that* Liberty, languishing as it *is*.

AN INDIAN is placed on the Pedestal; in an *erect* Posture, with an attentive Countenance, watching, as AMERICA has done for Five Years past, the extraordinary Motions of the BRITISH Senate——He listens to the Orator, and has a Bow in his Hand, and a Dog by his Side, to shew the natural *Faithfulness and Firmness of* AMERICA.

IT was advised by some, to have had the INDIAN drawn in a dejected and melancholy Posture: And, considering the apparent Weakness of the Colonies, and the Power of the Parent Country, it might not, perhaps, have been improper to have executed it in that Manner; but in Truth the AMERICANS, being well founded in their Principles, and animated with a sacred Love for their Country, have never disponded.

AN ALTAR, with a Flame is placed in the Foreground, to shew that the Cause of Liberty is sacred, and, that therefore, they who maintain it, not only discharge their Duty to their King and themselves, but to GOD. It is decorated with the Heads of SIDNEY and HAMPDEN, who, with undaunted Courage, spoke, wrote, and died in Defence of the true Principles of Liberty, and of those Rights and Blessings which GREAT-BRITAIN now enjoys: For, as the Banner placed between them expresses it,

SANCTUS AMOR PATRIÆ DAT ANIMUM.

A CIVIC CROWN is laid on the Altar, as consecrated to *that* MAN who preserved his Fellow-Citizens and Subjects from Destruction!

THE View of W——H—— is introduced in the Back Ground, not meerly as an elegant Piece of Architecture, but as it was the Place where ———— suffered, for attempting to invade the Rights of the BRITISH Kingdoms: And it is observable, that the Statue and Altar of BRITISH Liberty are erected near the Spot where that great *Sacrifice* was made, through sad Necessity, to the Honour, Happiness, Virtue, and in one Word, to the Liberty of the BRITISH People.

THE Petition of the Congress at NEW-YORK, and the Representation of W——H—— point out the Time, and almost the Place, where the Speech was delivered.

THE chief Object of this Design will be answered, if it manifests, in the least, the Gratitude of AMERICA to his Lordship. It will, with Tradition, unprejudiced by the Writings of *Hirelings*, who are made to glide in with the courtly Streams of FALSHOOD, be the faithful Conveyance to Posterity of the Knowledge of those GREAT THINGS which we, who are not to be imposed on by "the busy Doings and Undoings" of the envious Great, have seen.

Broadside [n.d.], by Charles Willson Peale.

George Washington Resigns as Commander-in-Chief

On December 23, 1783, George Washington came before Congress, meeting in the Old Senate Chamber, to resign his commission as commander-in-chief of the Continental Army. This occasion was, in many ways, the final revolutionary act of the American Revolution. As commander-in-chief of the victorious American forces, Washington was certainly the most visible, and perhaps obvious, person to lead the new nation. Many people in America and Europe thought he would retain the reins of power to become its leader, or maybe even its king. When told by the American artist Benjamin West that Washington was going to resign, King George III of England is purported to have said "If he does that, he will be the greatest man in the world."

Washington, however, had an abiding faith in the young nation, as well as a deep desire to return to his beloved Mount Vernon and his former life as a farmer. Congress had assembled in Annapolis in late November and awaited the general's arrival to resign his commission. He arrived in the city on December 19 and immediately wrote to Congress to inquire as to how they actually wanted him to resign. A committee of Congress, made up of Thomas Jefferson, James McHenry, and Elbridge Gerry, devised a ceremony that took place at noon on December 23. In the intervening days, Washington was feted with dinners and balls, including a gala ball on the night before the ceremony in the hall of the State House, where he is said to have danced with every lady present.

On the day of the ceremony, Washington arrived at the State House where Congress was meeting in the Old Senate Chamber. When he entered the chamber, the members remained seated and covered. In a brief, emotional speech, Washington resigned his commission and then bowed to Congress. Only then did the members rise and remove their hats in a gesture of respect. As he left the chamber to ride to Mount Vernon in time to have his Christmas dinner at home, Washington handed his personal copy of his speech to James McHenry. It is this copy that the state of Maryland acquired in 2007 from a descendant of McHenry, in whose family it had remained.

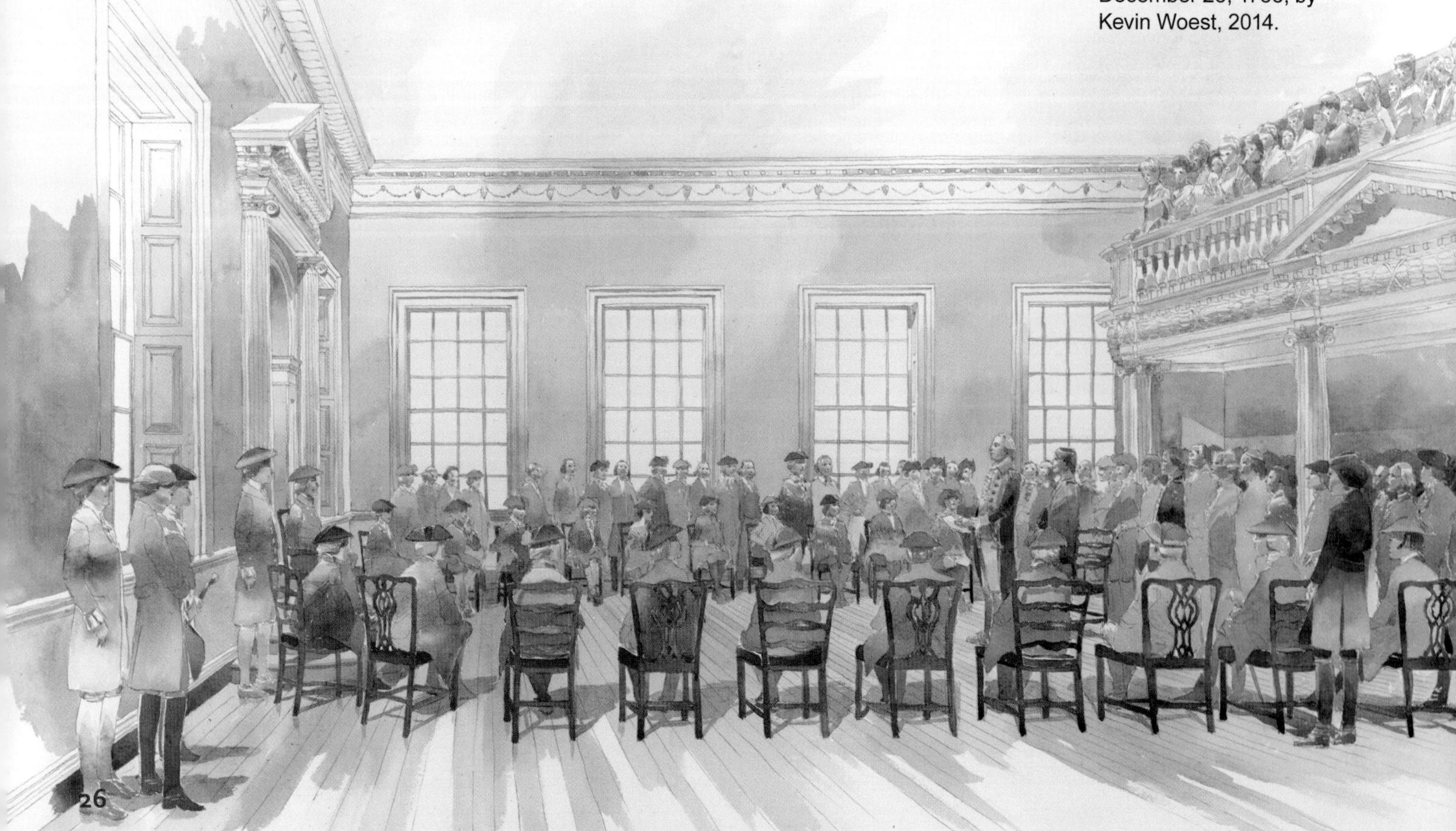

George Washington Resigning His Commission, December 23, 1783, by Kevin Woest, 2014.

Washington Resigning His Commission

By Edwin White, 1858

In 1856, the Maryland legislature commissioned a painting to commemorate the seventy-fifth anniversary of George Washington's historic act. *Washington Resigning His Commission* was completed in 1858 and was in the Senate Chamber until 1905. It now hangs in the grand staircase. A similar painting depicting the scene of Washington's resignation was painted by John Trumbull between 1822–24 and is on display in the rotunda of the United States Capitol.

Edwin White, a Massachusetts artist, was selected and paid $3,000. The frame was created by Baltimore craftsman Samson Carris, who received $300 for his elaborate and generously gilded work.

Mr. President,

The great events on which my resignation depended having at length taken place; I have now the honor of offering my sincere congratulations to Congress and of presenting myself before them to surrender into their hands the trust committed to me, and to claim the indulgence of retiring ~~request permission to retire~~ from the Service of my Country. —

Happy in the confirmation of our Independence and Sovereignty, and pleased with the opportunity afforded the United States of becoming a respectable Nation ~~as well as with the contemplation of our prospect of National happiness~~, I resign with satisfaction the Appointment I accepted with diffidence — A diffidence in my abilities to accomplish so arduous a task, which however was superseded by a confidence in the rectitude of our Cause, the support of the supreme Power of the Union, and the patronage of Heaven.

The successful termination of the War has verified the more sanguine expectations — and my gratitude for the interposition of Providence, and the assistance I have received from my Countrymen, encreases with every review of the momentous Contest. —

While

While I repeat my obligations to the Army in general, I should do injustice to my own feelings not to acknowledge in this place the peculiar services and distinguished merits of the Gentlemen who have been attached to my person during the War. — It was impossible the choice of confidential Officers to compose my family should have been more fortunate. — Permit me Sir, to recommend in particular those, who have continued in Service to the present moment, as worthy of the favorable notice and patronage of Congress. —

I consider it an indispensable duty ~~duty~~ to close this last solemn act of my Official life, by commending the Interests of our dearest Country to the protection of Almighty God, and those who have the superintendence ~~direction~~ of them, to his holy keeping. —

Having now finished the work assigned me, I retire from the great theatre of Action — and bidding an affectionate ~~[illegible]~~ farewell to this august body under whose orders I have so long acted, I here offer ~~surrender~~ my Commission, and take my ~~ultimate~~ leave of all the employments of public life. —

George Washington's Resignation Speech, December 23, 1783.

George Washington's Resignation Speech

Annapolis, December 23, 1783

One of the most important documents in American history

Mr. President,

The great events on which my resignation depended, having at length taken place, I have now the honor *of offering my sincere congratulations to Congress, and [&]* of presenting myself before {~~Congress~~} them, to surrender into their hands the trust committed to me, and to *claim the indulgence of retiring* {~~request permission to retire~~} from the Service of my Country.

Happy in the confirmation of our Independence and Sovereignty, *and pleased with the opportunity afforded the United States, of becoming a respectable Nation* {~~as well as in the contemplation of our prospect of National happiness~~},

I resign with satisfaction the appointment I accepted with diffidence—

A diffidence in my abilities to accomplish so arduous a task, which however was superseded by a confidence in the rectitude of our Cause, the support of the supreme Power of the Union, and the patronage of Heaven.

The successful termination of the War has verified the most sanguine expectations- and my gratitude for the interposition of Providence, and the assistance I have received from my Countrymen, increases with every review of the momentous Contest.

While I repeat my obligations to the Army in general, I should do injustice to my own feelings not to acknowledge *in this place* the peculiar Services and distinguished merits of the Gentlemen who have been attached to my person during the War. —It was impossible the choice of confidential officers to compose my family should have been more fortunate.

—Permit me Sir, to recommend in particular those, who have continued in service to the present moment, as worthy of the favorable notice *& patronage* of Congress.—

I consider it an indispensable duty {~~duty~~} to close this last solemn act of my Official life, by commending the Interests of our dearest Country to the protection of Almighty God, and those who have the *superintendance* {~~direction~~} of them, to his holy keeping.—

Having now finished the work assigned me, I retire from the great theatre of Action, —and bidding an affectionate {~~a final~~} farewell to this August body, under whose orders I have so long acted, I here *offer* {~~today deliver?~~} my Commission, and take my {~~ultimate~~} leave of all the employments of public life.

The words in italics were inserted by Washington as he contemplated his first draft of the speech. He also crossed out two important words, both relating to his leave of public office: a "final" farewell and "ultimate" leave. In doing so, Washington kept open his option of returning to public life. Washington also made a plea for Congress to pay the soldiers with whom he served and to fund the pensions of his officers, as they had been promised.

This speech is regarded as the fourth most important document in American history after the Declaration of Independence, the Constitution, and the Bill of Rights. The Friends of the Maryland State Archives purchased this historic document with funds from the state of Maryland, a tax deductible gift on the part of the owners, and two generous donations. It has been on display in the rotunda since 2015 in a specially designed case.

The Old House of Delegates Chamber

The Old House of Delegates Chamber has been restored to its 1876 appearance and now represents the high-Victorian aesthetic of the late nineteenth century, incorporating elaborate plaster-work accented by intricate decorative painting and stenciling. For the room to be suited for modern use, additional lighting and technological capabilities such as a projection screen, electrical outlets, and data connections were incorporated.

Many important events related to the expansion of rights in Maryland, especially in the nineteenth century, took place in this chamber. However, this space had been drastically changed over time, even divided into two rooms for many years. The existence of photo-graphs and furnishings associated with the late-nineteenth-century House of Delegates Chamber provided rich details of the exuberant polychrome paint scheme, lighting fixtures, desks, chairs, cornices, and even furnishing textiles of the ca. 1876 decor. The existence of original artwork in the state-owned art collection further enabled an accurate interpretation of this chamber.

The chamber was home for many years to the first, and most important, work of art ever commissioned by the Maryland legislature, a full-length portrait of George Washington. Immediately after the October 19, 1781 British surrender at Yorktown, Washington dispatched his aide-de-camp, Marylander Tench Tilghman, to Philadelphia to deliver the Articles of Capitulation to Congress. Washington then headed north and stopped in Annapolis from November 21–23, where he stayed with Governor Thomas Sim Lee. The entire town celebrated the American victory and honored Washington with dinners, dances, and entertainments.

On the day Washington departed, the House of Delegates appealed to Governor Lee to ask Charles Willson Peale to paint a portrait of him for display in the State House. Peale's resulting portrait sought to commemorate the American victory at the Battle of Yorktown rather than just provide "a mere coppy" of an existing portrait of Washington. To achieve this goal, he added the Marquis de Lafayette and Tench Tilghman to the portrait.

In October 1784, when it was completed, plans were made for its installation in the House of Delegates Chamber. Peale arrived in Annapolis on December 10, and assisted by cabinetmaker and State House superintendent John Shaw, assembled the frame and placed it in the chamber. The monumental portrait was received with great excitement. Peale presented his bill of £213.4.0 for the painting, frame, delivery, and installation to Governor William Paca on December 20, recording payment on the same day. *Washington, Lafayette and Tilghman at Yorktown* was the pride of the House of Delegates Chamber for almost 100 years. Still in its original frame, it is now in the Senate Committee Room.

The earliest changes and updates to the chamber and its furnishings were largely done to accommodate the rapidly growing number of delegates. As the House used a model of representation based upon population within the legislative districts, its numbers grew along with the state.

Top right:
Ornamental plaster,
Old House of Delegates
Chamber ceiling.

The "Jew Bill"

Thomas Kennedy, a delegate from Hagerstown, began his campaign in the 1818 session to provide Jewish citizens of Maryland with the same rights as the rest of the population. The Maryland Constitution of 1776 had set forth the requirements for holding an elected office: "No other test or qualification ought to be required on admission to any office of trust or profit than such oath of support and fidelity to the State… and a declaration of belief in the Christian religion."

Members of the Jewish faith were allowed to vote but could not hold elected office. The bill that Thomas Kennedy introduced in 1818 became known as the "Jew Bill," or, more exactly, "An Act to extend to the sect of people professing the Jewish religion, the same rights and privileges enjoyed by Christians." The bill was voted down several times before being passed on January 5, 1826. It amended the state's Test Act to allow members of the Jewish faith to hold public office upon swearing to a belief in "the doctrine of reward and punishment" rather than a declaration of belief in Christianity. In passing this act, Maryland became the last state in the Union to allow Jews to hold public office.

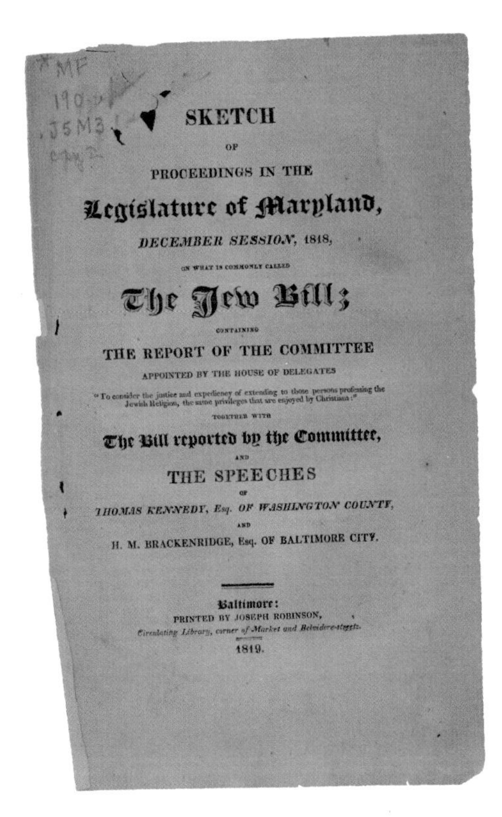

SKETCH
OF
PROCEEDINGS IN THE
Legislature of Maryland,
DECEMBER SESSION, 1818,
ON WHAT IS COMMONLY CALLED
The Jew Bill;
CONTAINING
THE REPORT OF THE COMMITTEE
APPOINTED BY THE HOUSE OF DELEGATES
"To consider the justice and expediency of extending to those persons professing the Jewish Religion, the same privileges that are enjoyed by Christians:"
TOGETHER WITH
The Bill reported by the Committee,
AND
THE SPEECHES
OF
THOMAS KENNEDY, Esq. OF WASHINGTON COUNTY,
AND
H. M. BRACKENRIDGE, Esq. OF BALTIMORE CITY.

Baltimore:
PRINTED BY JOSEPH ROBINSON,
Circulating Library, corner of Market and Belvidere-streets.
1819.

The "Jew Bill," Thomas Kennedy's first attempt to pass a bill allowing Jews to hold public office, 1818.

Enlarging The Chamber

As late as 1841, as noted in David Ridgely's *Annals of Annapolis*, the House of Delegates Chamber was the same size as the Senate Chamber "thirty-four feet by forty" and was "neatly fitted up, and accommodates seventy-nine members, who sit at desks conveniently arranged. It has also a lobby and a gallery for the accommodation of spectators, and with it are connected committee rooms." Also mentioned was the continued presence of the portrait *Washington, Lafayette and Tilghman at Yorktown.*

During the major renovations of 1858, many of the improvements, including new steam heating and gas lighting, focused on this chamber. On March 25, an article in the *Annapolis Gazette* noted that:

> *… the House of Delegates is to be enlarged by the addition of the House Committee Room… This addition will make the Hall of the House of Delegates nearly twice as large as at present. Competent persons, having examined the intervening walls, have decided that the walls appear to have been built as though their removal had been anticipated. Consequently, the strength of the building will be in no wise [sic] impaired.*

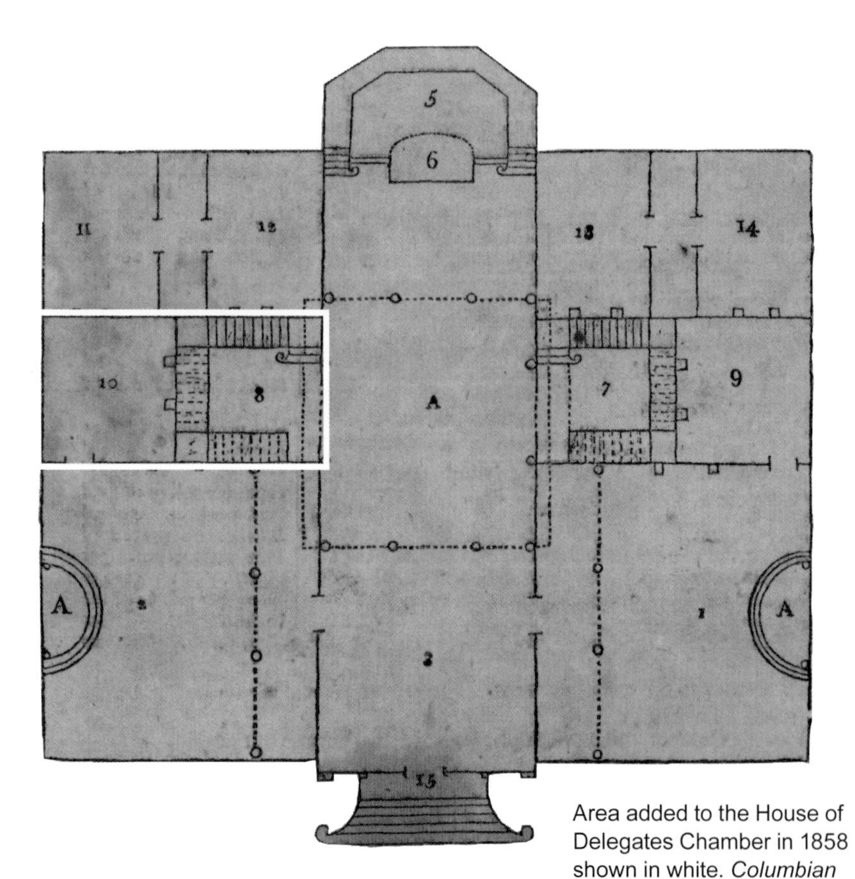

Area added to the House of Delegates Chamber in 1858 shown in white. *Columbian Magazine*, 1789.

Thomas Holliday Hicks (1798–1865), by James Kimball Harley, 1867.

The Civil War Years

In 1858, Thomas Holliday Hicks was elected governor. At the outbreak of the Civil War, with bloodshed in Baltimore during the Pratt Street Riots in April of 1861, Hicks refused to convene the legislature in Annapolis, which was occupied by Union troops. Instead, it met in Frederick, a Union stronghold but less likely to be a flashpoint of Confederate sympathies. Although always opposed to abolition and worried about Maryland's role as a border state, Hicks addressed the legislature, "The only safety of Maryland lies in preserving a neutral position between our brethren of the North and of the South." He eventually came to support the Union cause and helped prevent Maryland from seceding. A portrait of Hicks, by James Kimball Harley, now hangs in the Old House of Delegates Chamber in honor of his efforts to prevent Maryland from seceding.

President Abraham Lincoln's Emancipation Proclamation, of January 1, 1863, declared "that all persons held as slaves" within the rebellious states "are, and henceforward shall be free." If a person was enslaved in Maryland or any other non-secessionist state, the Emancipation Proclamation had no effect on their freedom. Maryland was still heavily reliant upon enslaved labor but Baltimore also had a large free-black population. The economy had shifted from labor-intensive tobacco growing to shipbuilding, and exports of wheat and other goods, but the state's 1860 census records indicate that 87,189 people were still enslaved in Maryland, about 12.5 percent of the total population.

Constitutional Conventions

As Lincoln's proclamation abolishing slavery only affected states in rebellion, it did not apply to Maryland; it took almost another two years for the state to emancipate its enslaved population. On November 1, 1864, the Maryland Constitutional Convention, meeting in the House of Delegates Chamber, passed a new state constitution that freed the enslaved population of Maryland with these words:

> *That hereafter, in this State, there shall be neither slavery nor involuntary servitude, except in punishment of crime, whereof the party shall have been duly convicted: and all persons held to service or labor as slaves are hereby declared free.*

The constitution also disenfranchised Marylanders fighting for the Confederacy or giving "any aid, comfort, countenance, or support" to the Confederate cause.

In 1867, the Maryland Constitutional Convention again assembled in the House of Delegates Chamber to create a new state constitution. The Constitution of 1867 remains in effect to this day with additional amendments. A number of noteworthy features of this new constitution include the assurance that slavery will never return to Maryland: *That slavery shall not be re-established in this State, but having been abolished, under the policy and authority of the United States, compensation, in consideration therefor, is due from the United States.* It also based legislative representation on combined black and white populations and gave African American men the right to vote in state elections.

Three years later, on February 3, 1870, African American citizens were given the right to vote in national elections with the ratification of the Fifteenth Amendment to the US Constitution. Huge celebratory events were held in Baltimore and Annapolis, including an appearance in Baltimore by Frederick Douglass, one of the most iconic figures of the fight for abolition and equality of rights. Another revered Marylander in this struggle is Harriet Tubman who was also born on the Eastern Shore. In recognition of their important roles in the history of Maryland and the nation, bronze sculptures of both Douglass and Tubman are in the Old House of Delegates Chamber. The statues celebrate the Maryland roots of these two pivotal figures in the nation's fight for the abolition of slavery and equal rights and justice for all Americans. The unveiling of the statues took place in February 2020 in a joint session of the Maryland legislature convened to honor these two historic native Marylanders.

A High-Victorian Redecoration

At the same time as the Senate Chamber was being completely renovated and redecorated by George Frederick in 1876–78, the House of Delegates Chamber was also undergoing its own high-Victorian treatment. Gas chandeliers and light fixtures were provided by Robert C. Cornelius of Philadelphia and new desks and chairs by the firm Harrington & Mills.

The earliest photographs of the chamber document many details of the room, including cornices and window treatments, and upholstery and drapery behind the rostrum. They also show the gas light fixtures, decorative painting on the walls and ceiling, and a portion of the highly-patterned carpeting. The room appears elegant and stylish for the taste of the time but it was clearly very crowded. By the 1886 session, the chamber had to accommodate ninety-one delegates.

In 1902, recognizing the desperate need for more space, the legislature passed an "Act to Provide for the Construction and Erection of an Addition to the State House." The previous additions, from 1858 and 1886–90, were removed and a new annex built between 1902–04. Baltimore architects Baldwin & Pennington designed and supervised the construction of the new annex, which now houses both legislative chambers.

Old House of Delegates Chamber, after 1893.

Harriet Tubman and Frederick Douglass

Harriet Tubman and Frederick Douglass were both born into slavery on the Eastern Shore of Maryland and escaped to freedom to become revered leaders in the fight for the abolition of slavery and equal rights for all Americans.

Harriet Tubman was born in Dorchester County in March 1822, although the exact date and place of her birth are unknown. Her name at birth was Araminta Ross. Like many enslaved people, she experienced a childhood of brutality and separation from family. In 1844, she married a free black man, John Tubman, and changed her name to Harriet Tubman. In 1849, she escaped to Philadelphia to freedom. She soon returned to Maryland to free her family members; in a total of thirteen trips, she brought some seventy enslaved people to freedom. During the Civil War, she was a nurse, cook, spy, and scout for the Union Army. Later in life, Tubman was an advocate for women's suffrage. She died in Auburn, New York in 1913.

Harriet Tubman and *Frederick Douglass*, by StudioEIS, 2019.

Like Harriet Tubman, Frederick Douglass's exact date of birth in February 1818 is unknown but he chose to celebrate it on February 14. He was born in Talbot County and, as an infant, was separated from his mother and raised by his grandmother. At the age of eight, he was given to Lucretia Auld who sent him to Baltimore to work for her husband's brother, Hugh Auld. Lucretia was an important person in Douglass's life as she taught him to read. On September 3, 1838, Douglass escaped to freedom from Baltimore by railroad and steamboat. He eventually arrived in New York City and immediately sent for Anna Murray, a free black woman in Baltimore that he had met before he fled. They were married and settled in Bedford, Massachusetts. For the remainder of his life, Douglass was an ardent and effective advocate for abolition and social justice. He was a noted intellectual, as well as a very gifted orator and writer. He died in Washington, DC in 1895.

These statues of Harriet Tubman and Frederick Douglass were dedicated on February 10, 2020 in a joint session of the Maryland General Assembly. On that day, the doors to the Old House of Delegates Chamber to reveal the new statues were opened by descendants of Tubman and Douglass.

Two Historic Paintings From Maryland History

Two historic genre paintings were purchased from Maryland artist Francis Blackwell Mayer. *The Planting of the Colony of Maryland* and *The Burning of The Peggy Stewart,* are important works of art in the chamber that help to tell stories of early Maryland history. The first commemorates the settlers on St. Clement's Island, in what is now St. Mary's County, planting a cross on March 25, 1634 in celebration of their safe arrival. In addition to the settlers, the picture also includes the Native Americans of the Yaocomico branch of the Piscataway Indian Nation, who sold the settlers the thirty acres of land on which St. Mary's City was built.

In *The Burning of the Peggy Stewart*, Mayer captures the role of Annapolis patriots in the events leading up to the American Revolution. In October 1774, Annapolis experienced its own "tea party" similar to the one in Boston harbor in December 1773. The *Peggy Stewart* arrived with a cargo that included tea and the ship's owner, Anthony Stewart, paid the tea tax, thus violating the non-importation resolution that had been implemented by the patriots in protest. Under threat of harm to himself and his family, Stewart burned the ship and all of its cargo.

The Burning of the Peggy Stewart, by Francis Blackwell Mayer, 1896.

The Planting of the Colony, by Francis Blackwell Mayer, 1893.

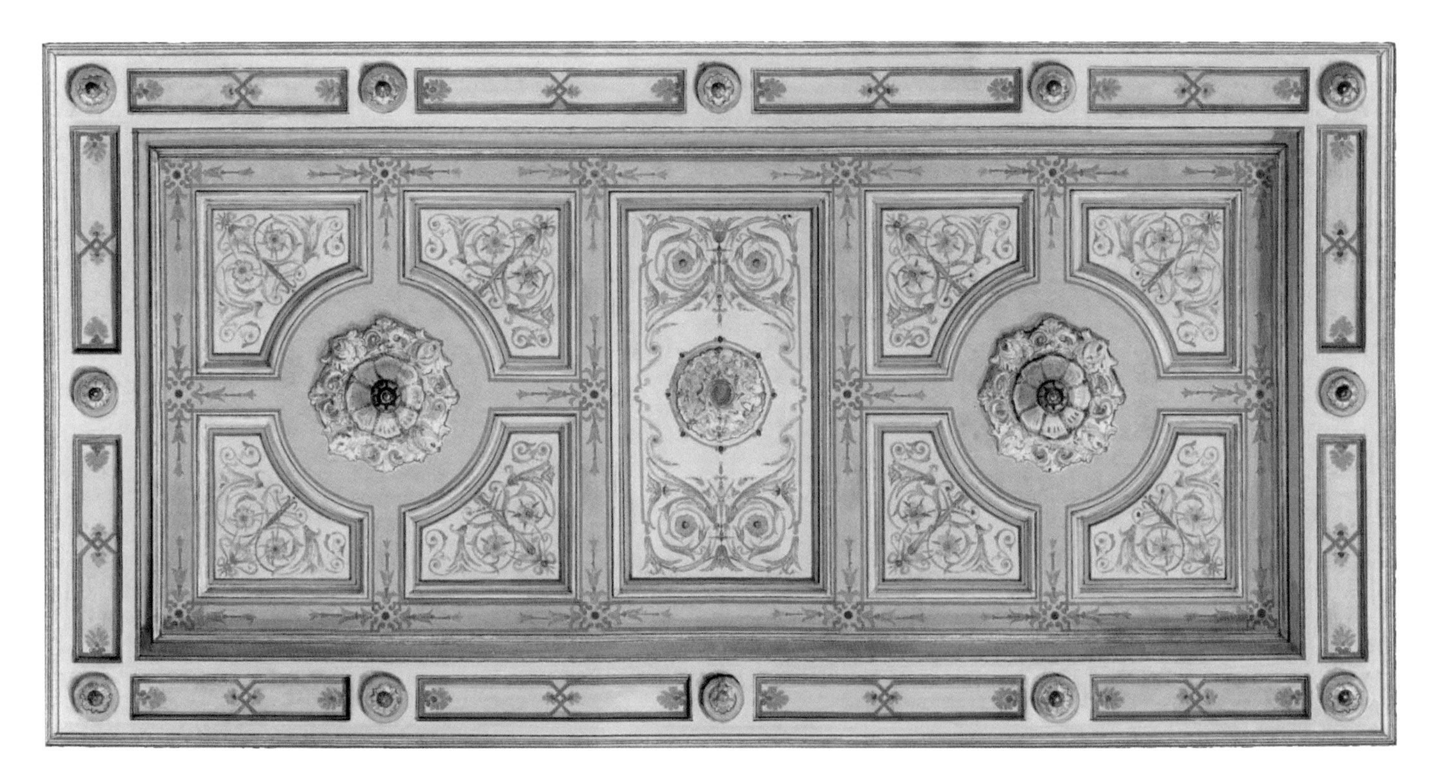

Design for ceiling plan, Old House of Delegates Chamber, by Beyer Blinder Belle, 2007.

The two houses of the legislature met in their new chambers for the first time in January 1904. While the state immediately set about restoring what was now the Old Senate Chamber to its eighteenth-century appearance, alternative uses were sought for the Old House of Delegates Chamber. One was for an exhibit by the Maryland Geological Society of the mineral wealth of Maryland, with a display of blocks of coal, marble, bricks, pottery, and tiles.

The adjoining room featured a display of the "Federal and Confederate flags returned to the State by the War Department." Throughout the twentieth century, the space was used for exhibits, offices for the Department of Legislative Services, and was repeatedly altered including dropped ceilings that destroyed the architectural history and detail of this once grand space.

As part of the research for the State House Visitor Experience Master Plan, preliminary investigation of what were then the Calvert and the Maryland Silver Rooms was undertaken to plan the renovations to the spaces. In 1998, paint analysis helped to guide the Maryland State Archives' 2005 proposal to the State House Trust recommending the restoration of the Old House of Delegates Chamber to its 1876 appearance.

This proposal called for the removal of the 1968 partition wall, restoring the dimensions of the room to its mid-to-late-nineteenth-century footprint. The choice of this time period allowed for the interpretation of the state's rich nineteenth-century history and the advancement of civil rights through legislation debated and adopted in the room. The Department of General Services, the Maryland Historical Trust, and the Maryland State Archives worked together to develop an accurate Historic Furnishings Plan and to re-create the Old House of Delegates Chamber as it was designed by George Frederick in 1876.

"I take the earliest opportunity to inform Congress of my arrival in this City, with the intention of asking leave to resign the Commission I have the honor of holding in their Service."
GEORGE WASHINGTON
TO CONGRESS
DECEMBER 20, 1783
"...the Gallery full of Ladies, the General seem'd so much affected himself that everybody felt for him...I think the World never produced a greater man & very few so good."
MOLLY RIDOUT
to ANNE TASKER OGLE
JANUARY 16, 1784

The Committee and Stairwell Rooms

These two rooms, adjacent to the Old Senate Chamber, feature exhibits that interpret in greater detail the events of December 1783–January 1784. The Committee Room, where Thomas Jefferson met with James McHenry and Elbridge Gerry to plan the protocol for George Washington's resignation ceremony, shows portraits of the people known to have been at the ceremony, as well as other Marylanders who were contemporary to the events. On the opposite wall a mural depicts the resignation scene in the next room, the Old Senate Chamber, created in 2014 specifically for this space.

Over the fireplace is the historic painting *Washington, Lafayette and Tilghman at Yorktown* painted by Charles Willson Peale in 1784, showing Washington with the Marquis de Lafayette and Maryland native Tench Tilghman after the British surrender at the Battle of Yorktown.

The Stairwell Room takes its name from the two staircases that dominate the space. The one on the right leads to what was known as the ladies' balcony where women in the eighteenth and nineteenth centuries were required to go in order to watch events in the Senate Chamber. Molly Ridout is shown on her way to the balcony to witness Washington's resignation. On the left is the "stairwell to nowhere" that once led to the second floor and an entrance to the dome and a jury room. Shown on the staircase is Thomas Jefferson ascending into the dome in September 1790 with James Madison, Thomas Lee Shippen, and a local doctor, John Shaaff, to admire the view and gossip about the local residents.

Molly Ridout ascends to ladies' balcony.

Thomas Jefferson and James Madison going up into dome.

Quotes and images on each wall address the following themes:

- **George Washington:** Highlights George Washington's journey throughout the war, from his appointment as commander-in-chief of the Continental Army to his resignation;
- **The Eighteenth-Century State House:** Features crucial events and original documents related to the Maryland State House in the eighteenth century;
- **Revolutionary Annapolis:** Shows the revolutionary fervor in Annapolis and early depictions of Maryland's four signers of the Declaration of Independence;
- **The Treaty of Paris at Annapolis:** Features the ratification of the Treaty of Paris, Thomas Jefferson's appointment as minister plenipotentiary, and Jefferson and Madison's visit to the dome in 1790.

Washington, Lafayette and Tilghman at Yorktown

By Charles Willson Peale, 1784

On October 19, 1781, British General Charles Cornwallis surrendered to General George Washington at Yorktown, Virginia, effectively ending the Revolutionary War. Following the victory, Washington dispatched his aide-de-camp, Marylander Tench Tilghman, to Philadelphia to deliver the Articles of Capitulation to Congress. Washington then headed north and stopped in Annapolis from November 21–23. The entire town turned out to honor him with dinners, dances, and entertainments.

On the day Washington left Annapolis, the House of Delegates asked Governor Thomas Sim Lee to "write to Mr. Peale, of Philadelphia, to procure, as soon as may be, the portrait of his Excellency general Washington, at full length, to be placed in the house of delegates, in grateful remembrance of that most illustrious character." In the end, Peale produced a large-scale painting that far exceeded the delegates' request.

In addition to Washington, Peale added two figures to his composition: the Marquis de Lafayette representing the alliance between colonial America and France that led to victory in the Revolutionary War and Lieutenant Colonel Tench Tilghman, pictured holding the 1781 Yorktown Articles of Capitulation and wearing his ceremonial officer's sword. A case to the left of the painting displays objects that had belonged to Tilghman: two swords given to the state by his descendants and a set of spurs on loan from the Maryland Historical Society. One of the swords is shown in the painting.

Senate Committee Room with painting of *Washington, Lafayette and Tilghman at Yorktown,* by Charles Willson Peale, 1784.

"...write to Mr. Peale...to procure...the portrait of his Excellency general Washington, at full length...in grateful remembrance of that most illustrious character."
MARYLAND HOUSE OF DELEGATES
TO GOVERNOR THOMAS SIM LEE
NOVEMBER 23, 1781
TENCH TILGHMAN'S SWORDS
WASHINGTON, LAFAYETTE & TILGHMAN AT YORKTOWN

U.S.S. MARYLAND SILVER SERVICE
U.S.S. MARYLAND SILVER SERVICE, 1906

The State House Caucus Room

The State House Caucus Room was originally divided into two spaces for the storage of records of the Land Office and the General Court. By 1841, the room was home to the Land Office, with an exterior entrance in the back corner of the room. Following the 1858 expansion of the Old House of Delegates Chamber, the rear half of the room served as the speaker's private office, while the front was a cloakroom for the delegates.

The room remained under the jurisdiction of the House of Delegates until completion of the 1905 Annex. In 1906, it was renamed the Flag Room and used to display the state's Civil War battle flag collection. A *Baltimore Sun* article from 1907 described the space as having a "great number of flags of priceless historic value," and noted that other objects, including ceremonial swords, were also on display.

By the 1940s, the space had been renamed the Bill Room under the jurisdiction of the Department of Legislative Reference. By the early 1980s, it was being used as the Maryland Welcome Center managed by the State Department of Tourism and continued to be used as such until 2008, when the space was transferred to the jurisdiction of the Maryland Senate, which used it as a meeting room.

In 2011, this room was redecorated and renamed the State House Caucus Room for use as a legislative meeting space. The room was recarpeted and decorated with a deep red velvet wall fabric, the color of the Maryland Senate, and is adorned with Maryland landscape paintings and portraits of nineteenth-century governors and legislators. The furnishings, including ten pieces on loan from the Maryland Historical Society, augment the display of paintings. At the far end, between the windows, hangs a portrait of Leonard Calvert, the first governor of the colony of Maryland. The room also features an exhibit of the USS *Maryland* silver service created by Samuel Kirk & Sons of Baltimore in the early twentieth century for the USS *Maryland* armored cruiser.

USS *Maryland* Silver Service

In May 1906, the citizens and school children of Maryland raised $5,000 toward the creation of this forty-eight piece silver service for the new USS *Maryland*. Made by Samuel Kirk & Sons of Baltimore, the set depicts 167 scenes from the history of Maryland's twenty-three counties and Baltimore City.

The USS *Maryland* silver service is unique. Not only do its pieces portray the houses, churches, and events of Maryland history, but their decorative borders symbolize the economy and culture of the state. Horns of plenty speak of hospitable, bountiful Maryland, "The land of pleasant living." Tobacco leaves and oyster shell borders symbolize the importance of both land and water in the life of the state. Rope borders on each piece represent the nautical purpose of the USS *Maryland*, and the names of twelve noteworthy Maryland naval officers appear on the punch cups. Each piece also features the Great Seal of Maryland.

On July 21, 1921, the US Navy commissioned the battleship USS *Maryland* to replace the original cruiser, and the silver service was transferred aboard the new ship. After twenty-six years of service, including duty during World War II, the *Maryland* was decommissioned on April 3, 1947. The silver service, which had been in storage during the war, returned to Baltimore. The silver was displayed at the Maryland Historical Society until 1962, when it was placed on permanent display in the State House.

On June 3, 1992, the Ohio-class ballistic submarine, USS *Maryland* (SSBN-732), was commissioned and four pieces of the Maryland silver service were placed aboard her as a memorial to the distinguished service of the two previous vessels of that name.

The silver service is made up of the following pieces:

St. Mary's County water pitcher.

- Allegany County filet platter
- Anne Arundel County centerpiece and plateau
- Baltimore City and County punch bowl, plateau, ladle, and cups
- Caroline County compote dish
- Carroll County asparagus dish and fork
- Calvert County coffee pot
- Cecil County fish platter
- Charles County cream pitcher and covered sugar bowl
- Dorchester County compote dish
- Frederick County game platter
- Garrett County candlesticks
- Harford County entrée dishes
- Howard County roast platter
- Kent County serving waiters
- Montgomery County ice cream platter and knife
- Prince George's County coffee waiter
- Queen Anne's County compote dish
- St. Mary's County water pitcher
- Somerset County gravy boat and ladle
- Talbot County vegetable dish and cover
- Washington County vegetable dish and cover
- Wicomico County gravy boat and ladle
- Worcester County compote dish

Anne Arundel County centerpiece.

John Shaw flag of 1783, as re-created, 2009.

Senate president's desk and chair, 1797.

John Shaw and the State House

In researching the early history of the State House, no figure stands out more than John Shaw. He was central to the appearance of the new building and its grounds. The desks and chairs from his shop for the Old Senate Chamber are revered as outstanding relics of eighteenth-century craftsmanship.

Born in Scotland in 1745, Shaw is believed to have immigrated to Annapolis in 1763, where he worked as a journeyman cabinetmaker. In 1772, he began a partnership with another Scottish immigrant, Archibald Chisholm, to form what became the largest cabinet-making shop in Annapolis. By 1776, he and Chisholm had separated to each form their own shops.

From 1779 onward, Shaw was closely involved in the preparation of the State House for its use by Maryland state government, including the two legislative bodies, the governor and council, and the courts. He was, in effect, the unofficial superintendent of the State House until his appointment to that role in 1794. One of his most important projects was preparing the State House for the Confederation Congress to meet in the Old Senate Chamber from November 1783 until August 1784. The flag he prepared to fly from the State House dome is still remembered as the John Shaw Flag and a copy of it was reproduced in 1983 for the celebration of the bicentennial of George Washington's resignation as commander-in-chief of the Continental Army on December 23, 1783 and the ratification of the Treaty of Paris on January 14, 1784. Another one of these flags flew over the governor's residence, Jennings House.

Well into the nineteenth century, Shaw was involved in major changes to the legislative chambers. These jobs included installing risers beneath the spectators gallery at the rear of the Old Senate Chamber as well as balustrades. He also provided carpets, blinds, ceiling repairs, and a decorative medallion. In 1797, Shaw was paid for providing twenty-four mahogany armchairs, ten mahogany desks, and a president's desk for use by the senators. Four of these original desks and five of his armchairs are in the state's collection and one is on display in the Old Senate Chamber. In the early 1940s, Baltimore craftsman Enrico Liberti was engaged to create reproductions of Shaw's desks and chairs for the chamber. Two of these armchairs and a desk are on display in a hallway outside the Senate Lounge.

MARYLAND STATE HOUSE
FOUR CENTURIES OF HISTORY
THE STATE HOUSE DOME
STATE CIRCLE

The Archives Room

The Archives Room marks what was, at the time, the northwest corner of the eighteenth-century State House. When the capital moved from St. Mary's City to Annapolis in 1695, transporting the records was an important part of the process, requiring bags covered in hides and sealed with the Great Seal of the province, and well-manned boats to cross the Patuxent River.

During the next 150 years or so, the records were stored in any space that could be found, including in the dome. There was constant danger of loss through fire, theft, and damp. Finally, in 1854, a select committee of the House of Delegates was tasked with inquiring "into the expediency of erecting a house for storing fuel, and a fireproof building for the preservation of the Records of the State... ." The result was the Archives Room that, in 1858, was made more secure in case of fire with a vaulted ceiling and brick floor. This space served as the main depository for state records until 1935, when the records were moved to their own, specially built, State Archives building on the St. John's College campus. This was done as part of the celebration of the 300th anniversary of Maryland's founding.

This building was the home of the state's records until 1986 when a new State Archives building opened on Rowe Boulevard, as part of the celebration of the 350th anniversary of the founding of the colony. Also for that anniversary, this room was restored to its mid-nineteenth century appearance. The 1935 archives building on St. John's College campus is now the Greenfield Library of the college.

The exhibits in this room are devoted to a number of themes related to the state's history:

- The early State House and the evolution of the buildings within State Circle, including the two earlier State Houses built before the present one and the many changes which have been made since its completion. It also describes other buildings on State Circle, including the Old Treasury Building, which was built between 1735–36 and is the oldest public building in Annapolis;

- The historic furnishings of the Old Senate and Old House of Delegates Chambers with examples of nineteenth-century chairs and desks created for the chambers;

- The history of the State House dome, with a cross-section model of the dome showing its construction of cypress beams and assembly with wooden pegs;

- A bust of Benjamin Franklin, who was the force behind the design of the building's lightning rod, which has protected the State House for 230 years;

- A tribute to Thurgood Marshall, a Maryland native who was the first African American to serve on the US Supreme Court. The maquette is a miniature of the statue designed as part of the Marshall memorial on Lawyers Mall, installed in 1996.

Rotunda of State House showing staircase to State Library, before removal of two nineteenth-century annexes, 1892.

The 19th-Century State House

EXPANSION & RENOVATION

The nineteenth century witnessed significant changes to the State House, many of which have been removed over the ensuing years. At times, there were serious concerns as to the structural integrity of the building, as well as an enduring need for more space. To meet that need, two annexes were added to the building, one in 1858–63 and the other in 1886–90.

The first major project of the century began in 1858 with an initial appropriation of $50,000 for improvements. The original small bay on the north side of the building was removed and replaced with a larger bay to house the State Library, which had been established in 1834. The entrance to this new bay was a grand staircase from the lobby. In addition, the House of Delegates Chamber was enlarged to accommodate the growing number of delegates, and the Land Office building on the grounds was built.

Two very important upgrades to the comfort of the people working in the building at this time were the installation of steam heat and indoor plumbing. A steam plant was built on the grounds and many of the fireplaces in the building were removed, including those in the Senate and House Chambers. The "public temple," or privy, next to the State House was also removed.

By the 1870s, the State House was in very poor structural condition and there were concerns that the ceiling of the second floor might collapse as had happened in the Virginia State capitol in 1870 when the floor of the Court of Appeals collapsed into the House of Delegates Chamber below. Sixty-two people were killed and 251 people injured. Such a highly-publicized tragedy made Marylanders more concerned about the condition of their own State House and influenced the extent of the work determined necessary, despite the nearly $100,000 cost overrun. Baltimore architect, George Frederick, was hired to assess the condition of the structure and make necessary repairs. The result of his work was the complete redecoration of both the Old Senate Chamber and the Old House of Delegates Chamber.

In 1882, the legislature turned its attention to the exterior of the State House and its grounds. The entrance to the building was enlarged and improved in 1882 with a new portico, cased in marble, with marble steps. The columns were of white pine and the cornice a duplicate of 'the old work', as was the door. This was, for most of the life of the State House, the main entrance to the building; it is now used only as an exit. The iron fencing around the grounds was removed, the hill graded, and new "parterres and pavillions" added as well as new walkways around the circle. The steam house that had been built in 1858 was removed, and the steam boilers moved to a new cellar dug a few years earlier, a change that greatly improved the heating in the building. As part of this heating project, two chimneys were added to the State House roof, where they remained until 1974.

Also in 1881–82, more work was done in the building itself. The black and white tiles on the first floor of the rotunda were installed by Hugh Sisson & Sons of Baltimore. Sisson was also the sculptor who created the fireplace for the former governor's residence, Jennings House, which is now in the governor's office. Four new columns were also added to the rotunda and the space was given new plastering and paint.

The second major addition to the building, which began in 1886, involved the addition of a second annex attached to the one built for the State Library in 1858. Primarily for the use of the library, this rectangular addition, connected to the earlier annex by a passageway, was quickly found to be unsuited for the purpose for which it was built and very poorly constructed. It was torn down in 1902 to make way for the present annex.

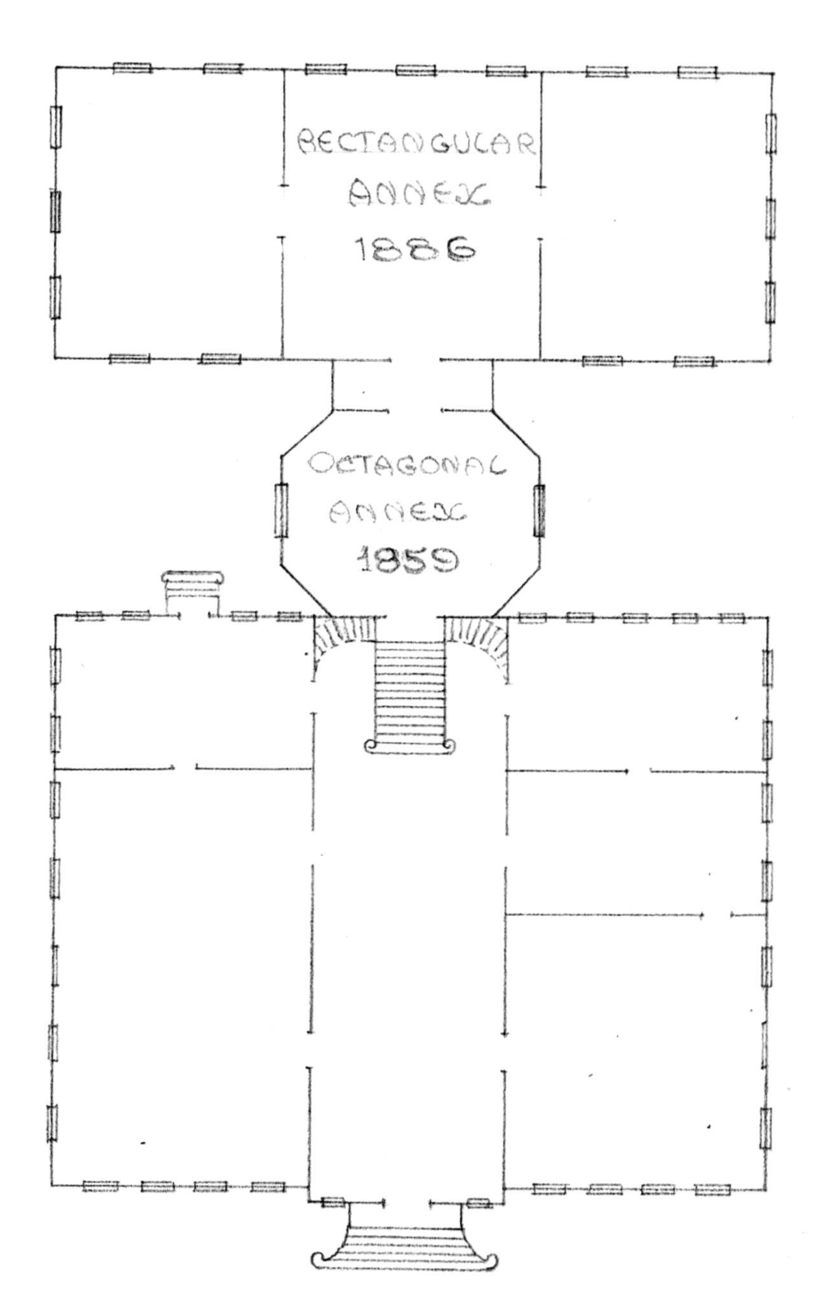

Floor plan showing both annexes built in nineteenth century and removed for present annex in early twentieth century.

Left:
Portico after enlargement in 1882.

Bottom:
State House before 1882 when fencing removed and portico enlarged.

Dedication of statue of de Kalb on July 16, 1886.

Throughout the nineteenth century, the State House housed several state courts: the Court of Appeals, the General Court, and the Court of Chancery. The Court of Appeals was located in the southeast corner of the building, in space that is presently used by executive department staff. What is now the office of the assistants to the governor was one of two jury rooms on the second floor. At the same time as the new annex was built in the early twentieth century, a new building for the Court of Appeals and other state agencies was built on what is now Lawyers Mall. That building was torn down in 1973, and the Courts of Appeal (Appeals and Special Appeals) are housed on Rowe Boulevard, across from the State Archives building.

During the nineteenth century, two statues were added to the grounds: Roger Brooke Taney, which was installed in 1872 and removed in 2017, and Johann de Kalb, which was dedicated in 1886. The fountain, pictured left, had occupied the space where de Kalb was placed.

View of State House, with first 1858 annex for State Library, and Government House on left.

A Victorian State House

By the end of the nineteenth century, much of the interior of the State House was decorated in the high-Victorian style that was fashionable at the time. The early-twentieth-century addition of the new annex also prompted the restoration of the Old Senate Chamber to its appearance when Congress met there in 1783–84. The Old House of Delegates Chamber was used as office and exhibit space.

Top:
The Court of Appeals on second floor, space now used as staff offices for Executive Department, 1887–1905.

Middle:
Old Senate Chamber after redecoration in Victorian style, 1878.

Bottom:
Old House of Delegates Chamber after Victorian redecoration, 1878.

HOUSE CHAMBER

The 20th-Century Annex

NEW LEGISLATIVE CHAMBERS

A black limestone line embedded with fossils marks the division between the eighteenth-century portion of the State House and the new annex built in the early years of the twentieth century. At the turn of the century, the state legislature was poised to make significant changes to the State House, as well as to spaces in and around State Circle. In 1900, it appropriated funds for the purchase of land for a new building to accommodate the Court of Appeals and the State Library, which were then housed in the State House, as well as the comptroller and treasurer's offices, which were in the Land Office that had been built on the grounds in 1859. A commission was established to select the site of the new building for the Court of Appeals and manage its construction.

The result of their work was the Court of Appeals building on Bladen Street and the destruction of the Land Office. This new building housed not only the Court of Appeals and the commissioner of the Land Office and the office of the comptroller, but also the tax commissioner, the State Library, and several minor agencies. After the Court of Appeals building was completed, regrets were expressed that the state had not bought enough land to set it back far enough to allow for a garden between it and Government House. This wish was finally realized when this building was torn down in the early 1970s to make way for what is now Lawyers Mall. For the State House itself, both the annexes of 1858 and 1886–90 were torn down to make way for the new annex that is still in use today.

The Baltimore firm of Baldwin & Pennington was engaged to design the new annex, with Josias Pennington as the primary architect. The builder was Henry Smith & Sons, also of Baltimore. The new annex houses both the Senate and House of Delegates Chambers as well as the offices of the president and the speaker and lounges for members of both houses behind their chambers. On the lower level, there are offices for the legislature and the governor's staff as well as space for members of the press. The second floor of the annex also has office space.

At the entrance to the annex is a remarkable set of bronze doors, each with one side of the Great Seal of Maryland the central feature, executed in high relief. They were designed by Baldwin & Pennington with assistance from the Maryland Historical Society.

The marble used in the legislative chambers was specially imported from Italy to reflect the black and gold of the Maryland state flag. Another important feature of the annex is the five skylights designed and made by the studio of Louis Comfort Tiffany. There are large Tiffany skylights in the House and Senate Chambers, as well as one over the main staircase and two more in the lobbies on the first and second floors. On the landing is the painting of *Washington Resigning His Commission*, as well as portraits of the last two Lords Baltimore: Charles and Frederick Calvert.

Left:
Bladen Street, showing new annex to State House, with Court of Appeals on left and Government House on right. Court of Appeals demolished in 1973.

Right:
New annex soon after completion, 1905.

Once the new annex was completed, the commission turned its attention to the condition of the original portion of the State House and found it to be in dire shape, much as it had been in the 1870s, with rotten floors and beams. As the new annex was fireproof, it was recommended that all of the beams and floors of the eighteenth-century part of the building be replaced to make it fireproof as well. In fact, it was in such poor condition that the reception for the inauguration of Governor Edwin Warfield in 1904 was held in the Old Senate Chamber rather than on the second floor.

Of even more concern was the condition of the dome and the commission recommended that the wooden dome be replaced with a new, steel dome of the same proportions as the old one. The General Assembly took a different view and directed that $1,625,000 in bonds be issued for the completion of repairs to the State House. This work included the restoration of the Old Senate Chamber that was overseen by John Appleton Wilson.

The Legislative Chambers

These two legislative chambers have been the home of the Maryland General Assembly since January 1904 when the legislators met in the nearly finished new annex. The skylights in both chambers were also created by the Tiffany Studios. Both chambers have galleries that are open to the public for viewing legislative sessions. The legislative sessions are held for ninety days every year beginning on the second Wednesday in January.

Behind the legislative chambers are offices for the president and the speaker and their staff members, and both chambers have lounges to which the members can retire while not in session.

Grand staircase with painting of *Washington Resigning His Commission.*

Verda Freedom Welcome (1907–1990), by Simmie Knox, 1991.

Thomas V. Mike Miller, Jr. (b. 1943), by Lisa Egeli, 2002.

Maquettes of John Hanson and Charles Carroll of Carrollton, models of statues in National Statuary Hall in the US Capitol, by Richard Brooks, 1905.

Senate Chamber, 1905–08.

The Senate Chamber

The Senate Chamber is where the members of the Maryland Senate convene during the annual legislative session. It features a skylight by the studio of Louis Comfort Tiffany, as well as Italian marble in the black and gold of the Maryland flag. On the side walls of the chamber hang portraits of Maryland's four signers of the Declaration of Independence: Charles Carroll of Carrollton, Samuel Chase, William Paca, and Thomas Stone. In the rear of the chamber are portraits of Verda Welcome, the first African American woman to serve in the Maryland Senate, and Thomas V. Mike Miller, Jr., president emeritus of the Senate, who served as president from 1987–2020. On the podium are maquettes of John Hanson, the first president of the United States under the Articles of Confederation, and Charles Carroll of Carrollton.

There are forty-seven members of the Senate, one from each legislative district. Until 1776, this body was known as the Upper Chamber of the General Assembly. Members are elected to four-year terms.

House of Delegates Chamber, 1948.

Each end of mace: Reverse of Great Seal of Maryland from 1794–1817, designed by Charles Willson Peale in 1794, showing tobacco hogsheads and leaves, sheaves of wheat, a cornucopia, and a ship, all symbols of Maryland's agriculture and trade.

The House of Delegates Chamber

Like the Senate Chamber, the House of Delegates Chamber features Italian marble in the colors of the Maryland flag and a skylight by the studio of Louis Comfort Tiffany. On the walls are portraits of speakers of the House of Delegates, beginning with the most recent one to have had a portrait painted. When a new portrait is installed to the right of the rostrum, all of the other portraits are rotated to the left and the one remaining is retired. There are 141 members of the House, three from each of the forty-seven legislative districts and each member is elected to a four-year term.

One of the most historic objects in Maryland is the mace of the House of Delegates. It is believed to have been given to the colony when its capital moved from St. Mary's City to Annapolis in 1695 by the royal governor, Sir Francis Nicholson. More than any other symbol, the mace stands for the orderly, deliberative process of representative government of the people, by the people, and for the people and is always on the rostrum while the House is in session.

The mace is a simple ebony or ebonized rod, 24.5" long and 1.75" in diameter. It is capped with silver on each end, engraved with the obverse and reverse of the 1794 Great Seal, which was commissioned by the state from Charles Willson Peale, and added to the mace. The motto, "Industry the Means, Plenty the Result," was the official state motto from 1794 until 1817.

Maryland's Four Signers of the Declaration of Independence

These four portraits honoring the four men who signed the Declaration of Independence for Maryland hang in the Senate Chamber of the Maryland State House.

Charles Carroll of Carrollton (1737–1832)
By Thomas Sully, 1834

Charles Carroll of Carrollton was the only Roman Catholic signer of the Declaration of Independence. He was a member of the Maryland Senate and was its president in 1783. He was also a US Senator from Maryland but resigned in order to retain his seat in the Maryland Senate. At the time of his death in 1832, at the age of ninety-five, he was the last surviving signer.

William Paca (1740–1799)
By John Beale Bordley, 1836

William Paca was governor of Maryland from 1782–85 and served in the Maryland Senate, as well as the Lower House and many other state and local offices. He also represented Maryland in the Continental Congress between 1774–80. John Beale Bordley was a Maryland artist who had studied with Charles Willson Peale. This portrait was painted in 1836, and the head is after one painted by Peale in 1772.

Samuel Chase (1741–1811)
By John Beale Bordley, 1836

Samuel Chase was a lawyer in Annapolis who held many local offices, as well as serving in the Lower House. He was an associate justice of the US Supreme Court from 1796–1811. The head of this portrait, which was painted in 1836, is after the 1811 portrait by John Wesley Jarvis.

Thomas Stone (1743–1787)
By John Beale Bordley, 1836

Thomas Stone was a lawyer who served in both the Maryland House of Delegates and the Senate. He was also a delegate to the Continental Congress for multiple terms between 1774–84. The head of this portrait, which was painted in 1836, is after Robert Edge Pine.

CÆCILIVS · ABSOL · DNS · TERRÆ · MARIÆ · ET · AVALONIÆ · BARO · DE · BALTEMORE
SCVTO · BONÆ · VOLVNTATIS · TVÆ · CORONASTI · NOS
MASCHI PAROLE

The Bronze Doors

The main public entrance to the State House is now through the doors of the twentieth-century annex, facing Lawyers Mall. These bronze doors, which have recently been cleaned and polished, were designed by Baldwin & Pennington of Baltimore, the architects of the annex.

Before they were installed on January 24, 1907, the doors were on display in New York City in the studio of John Williams, Inc. where they were cast. Their elaborate design, featuring the Great Seal of Maryland, was widely praised. Weighing 2,100 pounds each and measuring twelve feet high by eight feet wide, they required highly skilled techniques of the artist and the foundry to be created successfully.

The obverse of the Great Seal of Maryland shows Lord Baltimore as a knight in full armor mounted on a charger. The Latin inscription translated is "Cecilius, Absolute Lord of Maryland and Avalon, Baron of Baltimore."

The reverse of the Great Seal of Maryland shows an escutcheon, or shield, bearing the Calvert and Crossland arms quartered. Above is an earl's coronet and a full-faced helmet. The escutcheon is supported on one side by a farmer and on the other by a fisherman. It symbolizes Lord Baltimore's two estates: Maryland and Avalon in Newfoundland.

Memorials

A number of people in Maryland history are honored in the State House, as well as the committees and commissions that managed the many restoration efforts for the building over the years.

Matthew Alexander Henson (1866–1955)

One of the most notable plaques is the one honoring Matthew Henson, who reached the North Pole with Admiral Robert Peary in 1908–9. Henson was born in Nanjemoy, in Charles County, and grew up in Washington, DC. He was a true hero of early polar exploration and discovery. This plaque, dedicated on November 18, 1961, is the first state-funded memorial to an African American.

Rear Admiral Winfield Scott Schley (1839–1911)
By Ernest Keyser, 1904

This bust outside the House of Delegates Chamber honors Admiral Schley, a native of Frederick County and hero of the Spanish-American War. The General Assembly appropriated funds for this bust and pedestal in honor of Admiral Schley in 1902 and it was installed in the State House in 1904. It was cleaned and conserved in 2008. Admiral Schley is also represented on a silver punch cup in the USS *Maryland* silver service in the State House Caucus Room.

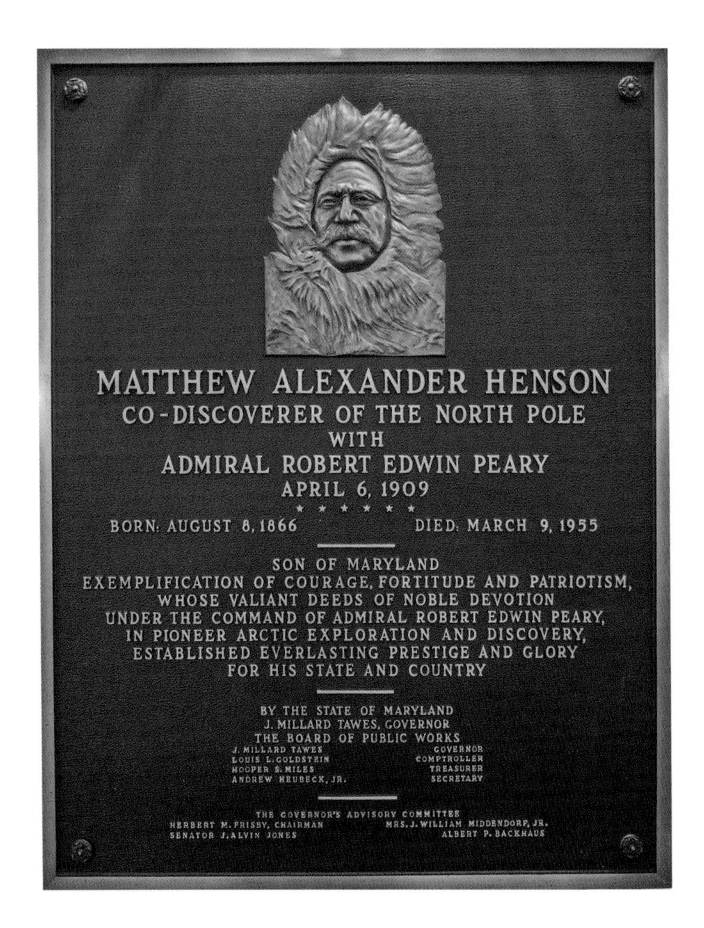

Thomas Johnson, Jr. (1732–1819)

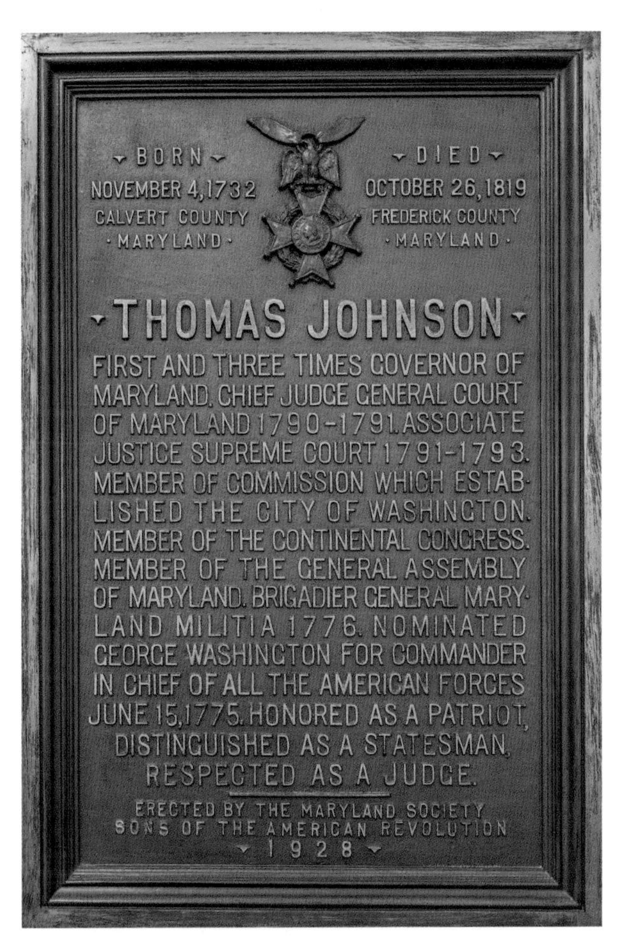

Thomas Johnson, Jr., born in Calvert County, was the first elected governor of Maryland, serving from 1777–79. He was a delegate to the Continental Congress from 1774–76 and was also an associate justice of the US Supreme Court from 1791–93, when he resigned. This plaque was given to the state in 1928 by the Maryland Society Sons of the American Revolution.

Right:
Thomas Johnson, Jr.,
by Charles Willson Peale,
1824.

Thomas Kennedy (1776–1832)

Thomas Kennedy was born in Scotland and immigrated to Maryland in 1793. He was first elected to the Maryland House of Delegates in 1817 and soon introduced a bill to allow Jews to hold public office, a right denied to them in the Maryland Constitution of 1776. The bill was defeated twice and Kennnedy twice lost his seat in the House. He was re-elected in 1825 and continued to pursue his campaign for the right of Jews to hold public office. The "Jew Bill" finally passed in 1825 and went into effect in 1826.

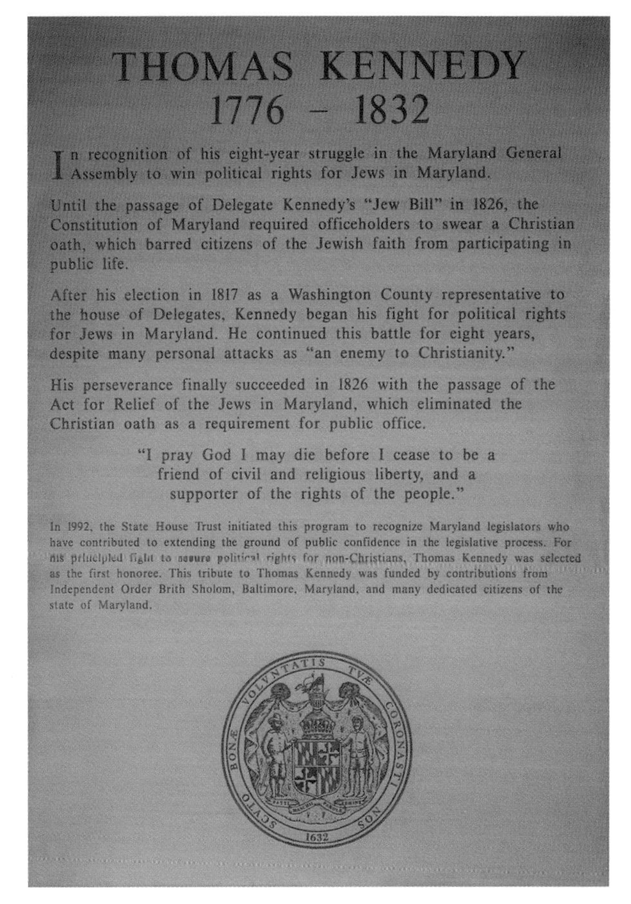

Maryland

The Executive Offices

GOVERNOR'S OFFICE & RECEPTION ROOM

Over the years, the space that is now called the Governor's Reception Room has always been associated with the office of the governor. A floor plan published in 1789 in the *Columbian Magazine* indicates that the large corner room (now the Governor's Reception Room) was then the Council Chamber, home to the Governor and Council, the state's executive body. The present governor's office served as a repository for stores and arms, while the middle room was a jury room. Between 1827 and 1835, the governor's office was used to house the State Library and, until 1905, it was the office of the adjutant general.

In 1838, amendments to the state's constitution replaced the Governor and Council with a popularly elected governor and established the office of the secretary of state. The large corner room became the public office of the governor, as well as the offices of the secretary of state and staff of the governor and the secretary of state. It was known as the Executive Chamber until the 1860s when it became the Governor's Reception Room. An 1861 House of Delegates order "to repair and fit up an Executive Office, adjoining the Executive Chamber in the State House" caused the former jury room to be set up as a private office of the governor. This marked the first time that a separate space was set aside for the use of the governor in the State House.

Before a private office was created, the governor usually conducted the business of the state from his office in his official residence in Annapolis. From 1776 until 1870 this residence was Jennings House, on what is now the grounds of the US Naval Academy. After Jennings House was sold to the US government in 1866 and the present Government House was built, the governor had his office on the ground floor of the mansion, immediately to the right of the front door, in what is now the Victorian Parlor.

Although the State House was enlarged and completely refurnished by 1904, the arrangement of the executive side of the 1772 State House remained unchanged. Offices of the adjutant general and secretary of state were relocated to the opposite side now used by the lieutenant governor. The relocation of the adjutant general allowed the governor to move his office to the less public space where it is now located. The center room became the office of the governor's private secretary, while the larger corner room remained the Governor's Reception Room, essentially the same arrangement used today.

The centerpiece of the governor's office is the Wye Oak desk, which was created after the historic Wye Oak fell in a storm on June 6, 2002. Estimated to be some 460 years old, the tree was the oldest and largest white oak in the United States and was declared the Maryland State Tree in 1941. The desk was constructed by the firm of McMartin & Beggins in St. Michaels, Maryland, employing traditional joinery techniques. Finishing details include an inset sheepskin writing surface embossed with the Great Seal of Maryland. The front of the desk opens to reveal a brass plaque inscribed with the names of the governors who have used the desk. It was installed in the governor's office in November 2004.

The Wye Oak Legacy

When the Wye Oak fell during a thunderstorm on June 6, 2002, it was mourned as one of the most historic trees in Maryland, along with the Liberty Tree on St. John's College campus in Annapolis, which had been removed in 1999. The Wye Oak, on the Eastern Shore in Talbot County, was some 460 years old and had witnessed all of the state's colonial and post-colonial history.

After the historic tree fell, several state agencies—the Departments of General Services, Natural Resources, and Agriculture—worked together to preserve the massive amount of wood that resulted. Among the many suggestions as to how the wood should be used was a new desk for the governor's office in the State House.

Wye Oak Desk in the governor's office.

To create the desk, cabinetmakers working in St. Michaels, Jim McMartin and Jim Beggins, were selected and some of the milled wood was moved to their workshop to dry, a process that took a year. Traditional joinery techniques, including hand-cut dovetails and mortise-and-tenon joints, were used throughout its construction.

Finishing details include an inset sheepskin writing surface embossed in gold foil featuring the reverse of the Maryland State Seal. A pull-out writing surface has the obverse of the Great Seal. The front of the desk opens to a plaque listing the names of the governors who have used it, as well as a plaque commemorating the Dorothy L. and Henry A. Rosenberg Foundation and the Rosenberg family who funded the creation of the desk. The design and construction were overseen by the staff of the Maryland Commission on Artistic Property of the Maryland State Archives. The desk was unveiled in the State House on November 18, 2004.

In 2008, a lectern for use in the Governor's Reception Room was made of the Wye Oak wood, also by McMartin and Beggins.

Victorian marble fireplace in governor's office, rescued from Jennings House.

Detail from Victorian fireplace.

George Washington, by Rembrandt Peale, ca. 1800.

Another important feature of the governor's office is the marble fireplace, which was rescued from Jennings House, the home of Maryland's governors for almost 100 years until it was sold to the US government in 1868. The fireplace was designed and created by Hugh Sisson of Baltimore in 1862 of Italian statuary marble with the Great Seal of Maryland in the center. Jennings House, which dated from the mid-eighteenth century, was used by the Naval Academy until its demolition in 1901.

Also in the governor's office is a portrait of George Washington, painted in about 1800 by Rembrandt Peale, son of the artist Charles Willson Peale. This painting came into the state's art collection when the state acquired the Peabody Art Collection from Johns Hopkins University in 1996.

TVÆ CORONASTI
VOLVNTATIS
BONÆ

The Governor's Reception Room

After the renovations of the early twentieth century, the offices of the adjutant general and secretary of state were relocated to the side now used by the lieutenant governor. At first, the Governor's Reception Room was used solely as the ceremonial public room of the executive department. To improve the appearance and to demonstrate the ceremonial function of this important space, Governor Edwin Warfield ordered the room be restored to its colonial appearance and that portraits of former governors be displayed in the room.

It was during the Warfield administration that the Governor's Reception Room was first used for bill signings. The Old Senate Chamber had previously been used for bill signings since the completion of the State House in 1779. The use of the Governor's Reception Room for this additional function may have influenced Governor Phillips Lee Goldsborough's decision to order the renovations and refurnishings of the executive spaces in 1914 and 1915. Under the direction of Governor Goldsborough, the room was furnished in a Colonial Revival style, and the four by nine foot table, now used for bill signings, purchased from the J. G. Valiant Company in Baltimore.

Portraits in the Governor's Reception Room now include previous governors of Maryland placed in chronological order around the room. When a new governor's portrait is hung, all of the previous governors' portraits are moved one space to the left and the oldest portrait is retired from the room and displayed elsewhere in the Annapolis complex.

The fireplace wall features portraits of the Calvert family. Over the mantel is a portrait of George Calvert, First Lord Baltimore, who originally requested the Charter of Maryland from King Charles I but died months before it was granted. To the left is a full-length portrait of Cecil Calvert, Second Lord Baltimore, who received the Charter in June 1632. Cecil Calvert organized the settlement of the colony but never traveled to Maryland himself. On the right of the fireplace is a portrait of Leonard Calvert, Cecil Calvert's younger brother, who sailed with the *Ark* and the *Dove* to Maryland to become the colony's first governor.

Queen Anne of England (1665–1714), by Michael Dahl, after Sir Godfrey Kneller, ca. 1702.

While the Governor's Reception Room itself features three members of the Calvert family, the entrance hall is adorned with three portraits of the British royals who played important roles in the early history of Maryland. The monumental portrait of Charles I was painted in the late eighteenth century in the style of Anthony Van Dyke, one of the most important European artists of the seventeenth century. It was Charles I who granted the Charter of Maryland to Cecil Calvert in June 1632, shortly after the death of George Calvert. Hanging beside Charles I is a portrait of his wife, Queen Henrietta Maria, after whom the colony of Maryland was named. This portrait was painted about the same time as that of Charles I, also in the style of Van Dyke. A smaller portrait depicts Queen Anne of England, after whom the city of Annapolis is named, as well as Queen Anne's County. These paintings were recently conserved with the support of the Sons of Colonial Wars and the Friends of the Maryland State Archives. They were installed in 2019 to reflect Maryland's royal heritage.

Governor's Reception Room, 1895–1905.

Governor's Reception Room, 1948.

The Governor's Reception Room, like the rest of the State House, has undergone many changes and redecoration over the years. The image from the late nineteenth century shows the room without a fireplace, as many were removed when steam heating was installed in the building in 1858.

Cabinet meeting in Governor's Reception Room, March 10, 2020.

TVÆ
CORONASTI

The State House Grounds

MEMORIALS & THE OLD TREASURY BUILDING

Over the centuries, State Circle has been home to several buildings, walkways, and even a large fountain that have all come and gone. When this State House was built in the 1770s, the circle already contained several existing buildings, including the second State House, which was built in 1704 and torn down to make room for the new State House. The Council Chamber, or the Armory, was built in 1718 on space next to the new State House and was removed in 1796. Also on the grounds was the "public temple," or "privy house," which was removed in 1858.

For most of the eighteenth century, King William's School, which was founded in 1696, stood on State Circle until it was torn down in November 1794. In 1784, the state had chartered St. John's College, merging it with King William's School, and the campus of that college has been across the street from the State House since 1784. Another building on the grounds was the Methodist Meeting House built ca. 1789 and torn down in 1817, as well as the Land Office, home to the comptroller and treasurer from 1859 until it was torn down in 1906.

The landscape of the grounds has undergone many changes and enhancements over the years. The first major improvement was a masonry wall built in 1818 to prevent erosion. By 1835, funds were appropriated to enclose the grounds with an iron fence and to construct gates at each of the three entrances. This granite wall with its fencing survived until about 1881.

With the exception of planting a few trees, the grounds did not receive very much attention until 1882, when funds were approved to improve the landscaping and paving of State Circle. The Board of Public Works advertised for a proposal and received two plans. It is believed that one of these plans was submitted by the artist Francis Blackwell Mayer, although there is little evidence that his was the one that was used. In addition to the improvements to the grounds, the project also included the replacement of the original, small portico at the front entrance of the State House with the larger one that remains there today. This is no longer the public entrance to the building, which is now through the annex facing Rowe Boulevard.

For 135 years, the front view of the State House was dominated by a statue of Roger Brooke Taney, a Maryland native and chief justice of the US Supreme Court from 1836–64. As the author of the *Dred Scott v. Sanford* decision of 1857, Taney has been a controversial figure in American history. The decision ruled that neither Scott, nor any other person of African descent, could claim United States citizenship, a divisive decision that is regarded as one of the causes of the Civil War. The statue was removed in August 2017.

EQUAL JUSTICE
UNDER
1908-1993

Thurgood Marshall Memorial

Unveiled in 1996, this memorial honors the celebrated civil rights leader who became the first African American to serve on the US Supreme Court. The memorial is placed on the site of the old Court of Appeals building where Marshall argued some of his early civil rights cases.

A native of Baltimore, Marshall graduated from Frederick Douglass High School and Lincoln University in Pennsylvania. He earned his law degree from Howard University in Washington, DC, where he first met the great civil rights lawyer Charles Houston. After earning his degree, Marshall returned to Baltimore and began his long association with the NAACP. In 1936, he won the case of *Murray v. Pearson* in which Murray was admitted as the first black student to the University of Maryland School of Law. In 1954, Marshall won the landmark case of *Brown et. al. v. Board of Education of Topeka et. al.* President Lyndon Johnson appointed Marshall to the US Supreme Court in 1967.

Following Marshall's death in 1993, the state decided to honor the civil rights leader and jurist with a memorial at the State House. After a nation-wide competition, the design of the memorial was awarded to Maryland artist Toby Mendez. Facing the statue of Marshall are statues of Donald Gaines Murray and two children, who represent the many children who were affected by *Brown v. Board of Education* case.

In 2018, the Thurgood Marshall Memorial was removed from Lawyers Mall in order to carry out a piping project. The statue of Marshall may be seen in front of the Courts of Appeal Building at 361 Rowe Boulevard, Annapolis. The entire memorial will be returned to Lawyers Mall in 2021.

Maquette of Thurgood Marshall on display in Archives Room.

Bottom left:
Statue of Donald Gaines Murray for whom Thurgood Marshall won admittance to University of Maryland School of Law in 1936.

Bottom right:
Statues of two children representing *Brown v. Board of Education,* which overturned doctrine of "separate but equal" in American public schools in 1954.

All by
Antonio Tobias Mendez, 1996.

Engraving from the *Columbian Magazine*, February 1789.

The State House Over the Centuries

This engraving above, published in the February 1789 issue of the *Columbian Magazine*, shows the State House soon after the completion of the dome. Two buildings visible on the State House grounds, the Council Chamber and ballroom, built ca. 1718, and the octagonal outdoor privy, known as the "public temple," have been removed over the years. To the right is the Old Treasury Building, built 1735–36, and to the far left is the John Shaw House, both of which still exist.

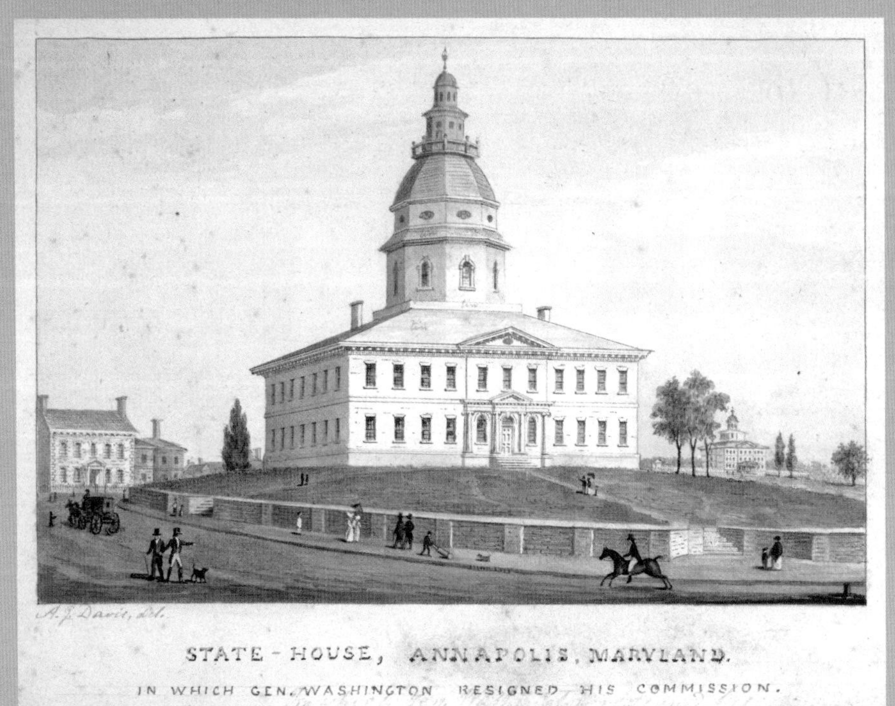

Bottom left:
State House, Annapolis, Maryland in which Gen. Washington resigned his Commission, 1836–40.

Bottom right:
State House showing rectangular annex built in 1886 and removed in 1902, by Elisabeth Ridout.

State House ca. 1900 with Land Office and Old Treasury Building to the right.

Land Office, built in 1858 and demolished in 1906.

State House, 1929.

Old Treasury Building today and before 1859.

The Old Treasury Building

The Old Treasury Building on State Circle is the oldest public building in Annapolis. It was built in 1735–36 by local builder Patrick Creagh. Originally known as the Loan Office, the building was used by the Commissioners for Emitting Bills of Credit who issued paper money for use in the colony. During this time, the building contained two iron chests for storing the bills of credit. Each chest had three locks and the three commissioners each had a key to one of the locks, requiring all to be present to open the chests. This office was abolished in 1779 and the building continued to be used by the Treasury Department until 1903.

In the early twentieth century, the Old Treasury Building was occupied by several different government agencies. In 1949, Governor William Preston Lane authorized a complete restoration of the building and Baltimore architects Henry Powell Hopkins and Laurence Hall Fowler were chosen to undertake the project, which was completed in 1951.

After the restoration, the building was used for a number of years by Historic Annapolis as a tour center. Extensive repair and restoration work has taken place, as well as archeological work around the outside of the building, which discovered the original grading and foundation work. More work remains to be done before it can open again to the public.

When reopened, as part of the State House Master Plan for the Visitor Experience, the Old Treasury Building will serve as a space to interpret early Maryland history, creating a link between Historic St. Mary's City, the first capital of the colony, and Annapolis.

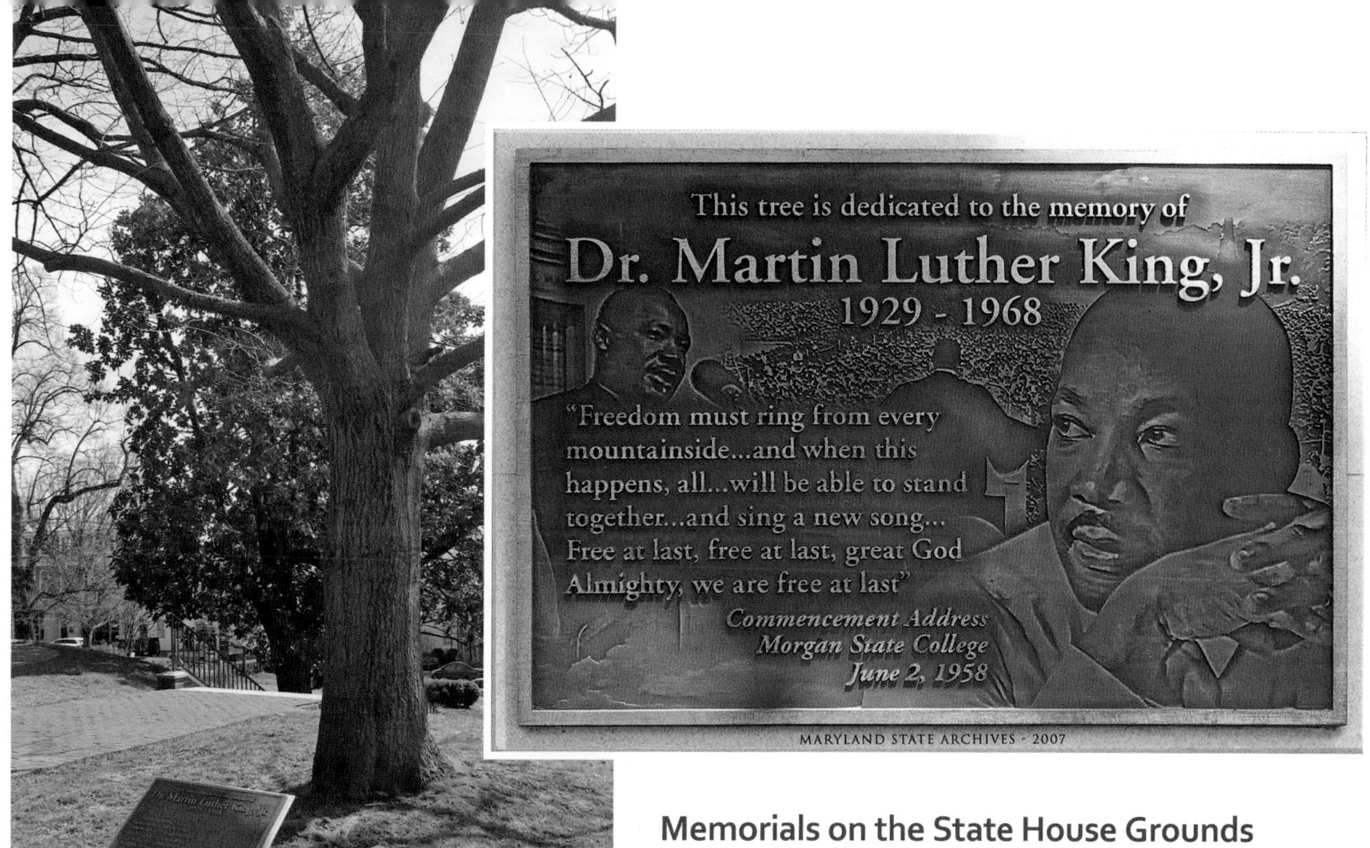

Memorials on the State House Grounds

Dr. Martin Luther King, Jr. Tree

This Northern Red Oak was planted in commemoration of Martin Luther King's birthday on January 15, 1984. The tree was rededicated on February 28, 2007 with a new plaque in King's honor. The plaque is inscribed:

> *"Freedom must ring from every mountainside... and when this happens, all... will be able to stand together... and sing a new song... Free at last, free at last, great God Almighty, we are free at last"*
>
> *Dr. Martin Luther King, Jr.*
> *Commencement Address, Morgan State College*
> *June 2, 1958*

USS *Maryland* Bell

This bell is from the USS *Maryland* battleship, which was commissioned in 1921 to replace the armored cruiser of the same name. The battleship remained in service until 1947. The bell was presented to the state and placed on the State House grounds in 1960. The USS *Maryland* silver service, which is on display in the State House Caucus Room, was used on both the cruiser and the battleship. A brass ship's clock with a provenance tying it to the USS *Maryland* armored cruiser was given to the Maryland State Archives. Records indicate that the clock, probably for the captain's quarters, was among the items included in fitting out the vessel in 1903.

St. Mary's City Cannon
This cannon came to Maryland with the colony's first settlers on the *Ark* and the *Dove* in 1634 and was mounted on the walls of the fort at old St. Mary's City. It was recovered from the St. Mary's River in 1822 and presented to the state in 1840. The plaque was placed by the Peggy Stewart Tea Party Chapter of the Daughters of the American Revolution of Annapolis on Maryland Day, March 25, 1908.

Methodist Church Plaque
The Old Methodist Meeting House was built on State Circle ca. 1789 on the site of a market house that blew down in September 1775 in a hurricane. This church, called the "Old Blue Church," remained on the State House grounds until 1817 when a new church was built on the corner of State Circle and North Street.

***Johann de Kalb* (1721–1780)**
By Ephraim Keyser, 1886
Major General de Kalb was a German soldier who fought for the colonies in the American Revolution. The statue was commissioned by the Maryland House of Delegates in 1817 in honor of de Kalb, who was fatally wounded at the Battle of Camden, South Carolina while leading the Maryland line in 1780. It has been on the State House grounds since 1886.

DeKALB

Reenacting George Washington's resignation as commander-in-chief, 2008.

Celebrating Maryland Day, 1987.

Celebrating Our History

Over the centuries, Maryland has remembered and celebrated the significant role the state, and Annapolis, played in the early history of our nation. Most important, of course, are George Washington's resignation as commander-in-chief of the Continental Army on December 23, 1783 and the ratification of the Treaty of Paris on January 14, 1784 which officially ended the Revolutionary War. That event made Annapolis the first capital of the new United States of America.

Other celebratory events include the annual commemoration of Maryland Day on March 25, honoring the day the settlers on the *Ark* and the *Dove* held their first mass in the New World. The anniversaries of these events have been commemorated with ceremonies, speeches, parades, and balls.

Bottom left:
Colonial ball in State House rotunda, May 15, 1928.

Bottom right:
Suffragettes gather on State House steps, March 1920.

Top:
Inauguration of Governor William Donald Schaefer, 1987.

Middle:
Celebrating 200th anniversary of Ratification of Treaty of Paris, 1984.

Bottom:
Child with statue of Frederick Douglass and The Extensions of Faith Praise Choir, celebration of Tubman and Douglass sculptures, February 15, 2020.

Governors

OF THE COLONY OF MARYLAND, 1634–1776

Governors of the Colony of Maryland, 1634–1689

Leonard Calvert (ca. 1606–1647), 1634–1644/5, 1646–1647
Thomas Greene (?–ca. 1651/52), 1647–1648/49
William Stone (ca. 1603–ca. 1659/60), 1649–1651/52, 1652–1656
Josias Fendall (?–by 1688), 1657–1660
Philip Calvert (1626–1682), 1661
Charles Calvert (1637–1714/15), 1661–1676, 1678/79–1684
Jesse Wharton (?–1676), 1676
Thomas Notley (1634–1679), 1676–1679
Benedict Leonard Calvert (1679–1715), 1684–1688
William Joseph (?–?), 1688–1689

Note: Men who temporarily ruled when the governor was absent from the colony, as well as in the period 1652–1657, when the Parliamentary commissioners displaced the proprietary regime, are not listed.

Governors under Royal Government, 1689–1715

John Coode (ca. 1648–1708/9), 1689–1690
Nehemiah Blakiston (?–1693), 1691–1692
Sir Lionel Copley (1648–1693), 1692–1693
Sir Thomas Lawrence (ca. 1645–1714), 1693, 1694
Sir Edmund Andros (1637–1713/14), 1693, 1694
Colonel Nicholas Greenberry (1627–1697), 1693–1694
Sir Francis Nicholson (1655–1727/28), 1694–1698/99
Colonel Nathaniel Blakiston (ca. 1663–1722), 1698/99–1702
Thomas Tench (?–1708), 1702–1704
Colonel John Seymour (?–1708), 1704–1709
Major General Edward Lloyd (1670–1718/19), 1709–1714

Governors under Restored Proprietary Government, 1715–1776

John Hart (?–ca. 1740), 1714–1715, 1715–1720
Thomas Brooke (ca. 1659–1730/31), 1720
Charles Calvert (?–1733/34), 1721–1727
Benedict Leonard Calvert (1700–1731), 1727–1731
Samuel Ogle (ca. 1694–1752), 1731–1732, 1733–1742, 1746/47–1752
Charles Calvert (1699–1751), 1732–1733
Thomas Bladen (1698–1780), 1742–1746/47
Benjamin Tasker (ca. 1690–1768), 1752–1753
Horatio Sharpe (1718–1790), 1753–1769
Sir Robert Eden (1741–1784), 1769–1776

Leonard Calvert,
by unknown artist, 17th century.

Governors
OF THE STATE OF MARYLAND, 1777–2020

Thomas Johnson (1732–1819), 1777–1779
Thomas Sim Lee (1745–1819), 1779–1782, 1792–1794
William Paca (1740–1799), 1782–1785
William Smallwood (1732–1792), 1785–1788
John Eager Howard (1752–1827), 1788–1791
George Plater (1735–1792), 1791–1792
James Brice (acting governor, February 10 to April 5, 1792)
John Hoskins Stone (1750–1804), 1794–1797
John Henry (1750–1798), 1797–1798
Benjamin Ogle (1749–1809), 1798–1801
John Francis Mercer (1759–1821), 1801–1803
Robert Bowie (1750–1818), 1803–1806, 1811–1812
Robert Wright (1752–1826), 1806–1809
Edward Lloyd (1779–1834), 1809–1811
Levin Winder (1757–1819), 1812–1816
Charles Ridgely of Hampton (1760–1829), 1816–1819
Charles Goldsborough (1765–1834), 1819
Samuel Sprigg (ca. 1783–1855), 1819–1822
Samuel Stevens, Jr. (1778–1860), 1822–1826
Joseph Kent (1779–1837), 1826–1829
Daniel Martin (1780–1831), 1829–1830, 1831
Thomas King Carroll (1793–1873), 1830–1831
George Howard (1789–1846), 1831–1833
James Thomas (1785–1845), 1833–1836
Thomas W. Veazey (1774–1842), 1836–1839
William Grason (1788–1868), 1839–1842
Francis Thomas (1799–1876), 1842–1845
Thomas G. Pratt (1804–1869), 1845–1848
Philip Francis Thomas (1810–1890), 1848–1851
Enoch Louis Lowe (1820–1892), 1851–1854
Thomas Watkins Ligon (1810–1881), 1854–1858
Thomas Holliday Hicks (1798–1865), 1858–1862
Augustus W. Bradford (1806–1881), 1862–1866
Thomas Swann (ca. 1806–1883), 1866–1869
Oden Bowie (1826–1894), 1869–1872
William Pinkney Whyte (1824–1908), 1872–1874
James Black Groome (1838–1893), 1874–1876
John Lee Carroll (1830–1911), 1876–1880
William T. Hamilton (1820–1888), 1880–1884

Governor Phillips Lee Goldsborough, Ellen Showell Goldsborough, and sons Phillips Lee, Jr. and Brice at Government House, Inauguration Day, January 10, 1912.

Edwin Warfield with Samuel Clemens (Mark Twain), May 9, 1907.

Theodore Roosevelt McKeldin with Queen Elizabeth, the Queen Mother, November 9, 1954.

Robert M. McLane (1815–1898), 1884–1885
Henry Lloyd (1852–1920), 1885–1888
Elihu E. Jackson (1837–1907), 1888–1892
Frank Brown (1846–1920), 1892–1896
Lloyd Lowndes (1845–1905), 1896–1900
John Walter Smith (1845–1925), 1900–1904
Edwin Warfield (1848–1920), 1904–1908
Austin L. Crothers (1860–1912), 1908–1912
Phillips Lee Goldsborough (1865–1946), 1912–1916
Emerson C. Harrington (1864–1945), 1916–1920
Albert C. Ritchie (1876–1936), 1920–1935
Harry W. Nice (1877–1941), 1935–1939
Herbert R. O'Conor (1896–1960), 1939–1947
William Preston Lane, Jr. (1892–1967), 1947–1951
Theodore R. McKeldin (1900–1974), 1951–1959
J. Millard Tawes (1894–1979), 1959–1967
Spiro T. Agnew (1918–1996), 1967–1969
Marvin Mandel (1920–2015), 1969–1979
Blair Lee III (1916–1985), acting governor, June 4, 1977 to January 15, 1979
Harry R. Hughes (1926–2019), 1979–1987
William Donald Schaefer (1921–2011), 1987–1995
Parris N. Glendening (b. 1942), 1995–2003
Robert L. Ehrlich, Jr. (b. 1957), 2003–2007
Martin J. O'Malley (b. 1963), 2007–2015
Lawrence J. Hogan, Jr. (b. 1956), 2015–present.

Top:
William Preston Lane, Jr. in governor's office, 1948.

Middle:
Senator John F. Kennedy and Jacqueline Kennedy with Millard Tawes, February 2, 1960.

Bottom: Left to right:
Robert L. Ehrlich, Jr., Parris N. Glendening, William Donald Schaefer, Marvin Mandel, and Harry R. Hughes, January 15, 2003.

101 Ranch cowboys in front
of State House, 1913.

Acknowledgements

While I am named as the author of this book, it is actually the result of many years of intensive research and writing about the State House by my colleagues at the Maryland State Archives. The sections on the Old Senate Chamber and the Old House of Delegates were primarily the work of Christopher Kintzel and Catherine Rogers Arthur for the booklet *Maryland's Historic Legislative Chambers*, published in 2019 for the General Assembly. Chris has also been especially helpful in checking facts and dates and finding images; his detailed knowledge of the history of the State House is remarkable. In addition, two former Archives staff members deserve recognition for their contributions to our knowledge of the State House and its history: Alexander (Sasha) Lourie, now associate curator for the United States Senate, and Michelle Fitzgerald, now curator at Homewood House in Baltimore. Our special collections staff, Maria Day and Megan Craynon, have assisted me in finding and identifying historical images.

This book would not have been possible without the guidance and support of State Archivist Tim Baker and Deputy State Archivist Elaine Rice Bachmann. Credit must also be given to now-retired State Archivist Edward C. Papenfuse for his enduring determination to document every aspect of the State House, its history, its grounds, and its historical significance. Finally, the Friends of the Maryland State Archives partnered with the Archives to fund the photography and design of this book.

Any reader who would like to explore the history of the construction of the State House in its many iterations over the years in great detail, including names of builders, payments made, laws passed, and controversies overcome, will find it all in *The State House at Annapolis*, by then-State Archivist Morris L. Radoff, published in 1972.

Most of the contemporary photographs are the work of our very gifted photographer, Medford Canby. Medford was for many years the chef at Government House while also pursuing his passion for photography. After his retirement from state service, we were fortunate enough to engage his skills for many of the images that grace this publication.

All writers need a good editor and I was fortunate to have several working with me, including my husband, Rodney Calver, and Jean Russo, PhD. My colleagues Catherine Rogers Arthur, Elaine Rice Bachmann, Christopher Kintzel, and Owen Lourie reviewed the text many times and have all been a constant source of inspiration and support.

And all books need a good designer with a sharp eye for detail. Michele A. Danoff, of Graphics by Design, is not only a pleasure to work with but is a wonderful designer with a gift for images and layout. She has designed many publications for us over the years and each one is a pleasure to the eye.

I also want to thank my friend, Willi Vogler of Zwingenberg, Germany, who has made great efforts to help me document a definitive connection between the Schlossturm at the palace in Karlsruhe, Germany and our State House dome. We are still searching!

Mimi S. Calver

Mimi Scrivener Calver

Mimi Calver is the executive director of the Friends of the Maryland State Archives. From 1991 to 2008, she was the director of exhibits, outreach, and artistic property at the Archives.

State House grounds before removal of Land Office in 1906.

Medford Canby photographing the interior of the dome, 2019.

Photo Credits

Unless otherwise noted, the images in this book are in the collections of the Maryland State Archives. Most of the contemporary photographs were taken by Medford Canby, except when noted.

Page 2: Courtesy of the John Work Garrett collection of the Johns Hopkins University, GAR 22

Page 10: Top photo: Bill Adair, Gold Leaf Studios

Page 24: Top photo: National Portrait Gallery, London
Bottom photo: Library of Congress

Page 51: Maryland Historical Society

Page 75: Joe Andrucyk/Patrick Siebert

Page 78: Brian Kutner

Page 79: All except maquette: Brian Kutner

Page 80: Bottom left: Albert Small Collection, George Washington University

Page 82: Top photo: Brian Kutner

Page 83: Michele Danoff

Page 84: Michele Danoff

Page 86: Top left photo: Tom Darden

Page 87: Top photo: Tom Darden

Page 90: Top photo: Courtesy of Jean Goldsborough

Page 91: Middle image: Bettman/via Getty Images

Page 95: Michele Danoff

Bird's Eye View of the City of Annapolis, Capital of the State of Maryland (detail), E. Sachse & Co., 1853–63